7

THE
PARALEGAL

Richard Deming

THE PARALEGAL

ELSEVIER/NELSON BOOKS
New York

Library of Congress Cataloging in Publication Data

Deming, Richard.
    The paralegal.

    Bibliography: p.
    Includes index.
    1. Legal assistants—United States.   2. Law—Study and
teaching—United States.   I. Title.
KF320.L4D45   340'.023'73   79-27172
ISBN 0-525-66655-9

Published in the United States by Elsevier/Nelson Books, a
division of Elsevier-Dutton Publishing Company, Inc., New
York. Published simultaneously in Don Mills, Ontario, by
Nelson/Canada.

Printed in the US.A.   First Edition
10 9 8 7 6 5 4 3 2 1

For Marc

Contents

THE PARALEGAL

Preface

Depending on where you live, the people this book is about are called lawyers' assistants, legal assistants, paralegals, paralegal assistants, or paralegal associates. Whatever their titles, they are members of a burgeoning profession of trained assistants who do legal work under the supervision of lawyers. They are not simply exalted legal secretaries, but a new breed of almost-lawyers with a much wider range of responsibilities than any secretary has.

For some reason, universities, colleges, and junior colleges use the term "legal assistant" more frequently than any of the other terms in their catalog listings of courses. That seems odd, because the commonest term used within the profession itself, even in many areas where schools graduate "legal assistants," is "paralegal." There are areas where some of the other terms are used, but across the nation the great majority of workers in the field call themselves paralegals, and most of their professional associations are known as "paralegal associations." A few are associations of "legal assistants," but none of them use any other terminology than those two. And one of the main organizations binding together the various regional organizations is The National Federation of Paralegal Associations.

Some paralegals were employed in law offices a decade ago, but only in very recent years has the profession begun to receive general recognition. By the early 1970's it had become widely enough recognized for the American Bar Association to form a Standing Committee on Legal Assistants to study the matter. In 1973 the committee held a conference at the University of Denver Law School to set guidelines for the training of paralegals. Out of that came a pilot training program instituted at four cooperating schools to test and evaluate certain standards set by the Standing Committee and approved by the House of Delegates of the ABA. In the short time since then about three hundred training programs have blossomed across the country. Between fifty and sixty programs have ABA approval, and many more are in the process of applying for such approval.

This book is designed to provide all the presently available information about this new career to those who may be interested in entering it. It is not an attempt to "sell" the career, but is meant merely to supply sufficient data so that the reader can make an informed choice. Both the advantages and drawbacks of becoming a paralegal will be probed. You will be told where you can obtain training, how long it will take, and what it will cost. You will be told what the employment opportunities are in different areas, and what pay to expect. You will learn what future trends in the profession will probably be, and what the long-range opportunities are.

I wish to acknowledge with thanks the considerable help given me by paralegal Linda Glasgow in arranging interviews for me with other paralegals.

R.D.

1

What Does
a Paralegal Do?

Because it is such a new profession, there is considerable difference of opinion as to just what the duties of a paralegal should be. The American Bar Association has issued only the vaguest of guidelines. No state has as yet passed any legislation defining what a paralegal is or setting standards of performance. Only one state bar association, Oregon's, has attempted to establish a certification program, and that has been a notable failure.

The National Association of Legal Assistants, headquartered in Tulsa, Oklahoma, has established a Certified Legal Assistant Program, which involves completing a two-day comprehensive examination. In 1975, it adopted a code of ethics for legal assistants. The American Paralegal Association, based in Los Angeles, issued a different code of ethics, also in 1975, and the National

Federation of Paralegal Associations, in Washington, D.C., has drawn up a list of the functions a paralegal may undertake. But none of the above organizations, including the American Bar Association, has any actual authority over paralegals anywhere. As a practical matter, a paralegal may perform any duties his lawyer employer authorizes him to perform, so long as they do not involve the illegal practice of law.

To date, the American Bar Association has not developed any standards for paralegals, although it has been considering doing so for some years. In 1975 the ABA Standing Committee on Legal Assistants held a series of public hearings throughout the country to determine the feasibility of certifying paralegals, and concluded that such action would be premature. That position was reaffirmed in August, 1977, and there has been no change in attitude since.

The committee did go so far as to state:

> Under the supervision and direction of a lawyer, the legal assistant should be able to apply knowledge of law and legal procedures in rendering direct assistance to lawyers engaged in legal research; design, develop or plan modifications of new procedures, techniques, services, processes or applications; prepare or interpret legal documents and write detailed procedures for practicing in certain fields of law; select, compile and use technical information from such references as digests, encyclopedias or practice manuals; and analyze and follow procedural problems that involve independent decisions.

That the committee draws a sharp distinction between paralegals and legal secretaries is made clear by its description of the duties of the latter: "The legal secretary should be prepared to take dictation by machine or short-hand; prepare fee and disbursement statements; prepare appropriate documents for real estate, probate, corporate, tax problems, civil or criminal litigation and domestic relations; keep books and records; and serve as receptionist."

The ABA Standing Committee on Ethics and Professional Responsibility has issued several opinions concerning the types of activities paralegals are permitted to perform. Opinion 316, dated January 18, 1967, says in part:

> A lawyer can employ lay secretaries, lay investigators, lay detectives, lay researchers, accountants, lay scriveners, nonlawyer draftsmen or nonlawyer researchers. In fact he may employ nonlawyers to do any task for him except counsel clients about law matters, engage directly in the practice of law, appear in court or appear in formal proceedings as part of the judicial process, so long as it is he who takes the work and vouches for it to the client. In other words, we do not limit the kind of assistants the lawyer can acquire in any way to persons who are admitted to the Bar, so long as the nonlawyers do not do things that lawyers may not do or do things that lawyers only may do.

Despite the judicial tone of the ABA's various statements, none of them makes clear what the organization thinks the duties of the paralegal should be. The ABA is very definite about the duties of a legal secretary, however, suggesting that the organization's vagueness about paralegals is because it does not really know what to do about them.

The National Federation of Paralegal Associations says:

The tasks and responsibilities of paralegals vary depending upon the areas of law and the level of experience of the individual paralegal. Paralegals may draft legal documents, organize and summarize documents, interview clients, interview witnesses, prepare correspondence and memoranda, perform factual and legal research, and perform other tasks as dictated by the needs of a particular legal matter.

Another definition, whose original source I have been unable to determine, appears in the brochures of many colleges and universities offering paralegal training:

A paralegal is a trained person who works under the supervision of a lawyer and functions as a member of the legal services team on a level between the lawyer and general office staff. Under the direct supervision of an attorney he may perform detailed legal research; draft briefs; conduct client interviews; draft wills and deeds, mortgages, contracts and instruments for property transactions; research and prepare corporate instruments; prepare pleadings and other court documents; research tax matters; handle aspects of probate and estates; research and analyze public records; conduct investigations; index documents for trial; supervise office management; and numerous other matters of equal challenge and importance.

As an example of what may be expected of paralegals in the public sector, this is the job description of a paralegal by the Colorado State Department of Personnel:

Nature of Work
This is highly skilled paraprofessional work involving the performance of a wide variety of paralegal duties requir-

ing the exercise of considerable independent judgment. Employees in this class assist attorneys with any of the paraprofessional legal duties required in an attorney's office. Employees receive limited general supervision from an attorney.

Distinguishing Factors
Positions in this class are distinguished from legal secretaries by incidental nature of the clerical duties of this class and the majority of the assignment being in either legal research, investigation, analysis or any combination thereof.

Some Examples of Work
Investigates facts and interviews witnesses statewide; evaluates credibility and weight of evidence; gathers other relevant evidence; analyzes and submits formal report of investigations. Reviews and analyzes legal briefs, memoranda, opinions and other relevant materials for points of law, digesting and indexing them for future references. Performs analytical legal research using Federal, State and local materials, administrative agency reports and other authorities. Determines the names and whereabouts of potential witnesses. Determines, prepares and collects copies of proposed exhibits. Composes correspondence and assembles necessary documents for own signature or signature of attorney by researching law, statutes, and previous cases and making decisions regarding relevance of research. Attends court to set cases for trial or hearing and continuance of cases. Assists attorneys at hearings and provides significant courtroom notes for use in cross-examination arguments and summary; performs emergency courtroom research. Files documents in the respective court systems. Prepares interrogatories and answers to interrogatories. Collects and evaluates legal statistical data for input into computer systems.

The above summary apparently authorizes the appearance in court of paralegals in Colorado, although such appearance is barred elsewhere, but it should be explained that "appearance" in the legal sense means representing a client in court. Paralegals may not do that in any state, but there is nothing to bar their physical presence in court to assist an attorney, so long as they do not attempt to speak to the court or jury on behalf of a client.

Phyllis Cardoza, a paralegal you will meet in the next chapter, says that a paralegal can do anything a lawyer can do except give legal advice, represent a client in court, or fix fees. Doris Peckner, another paralegal you will meet in the next chapter, likens her work to that of a British solicitor, although she emphasizes that, unlike solicitors, all of her work must be performed under the direct supervision of an attorney. In Britain there are two classes of attorneys: solicitors and barristers. Solicitors do the legal research for trials, prepare and file all necessary documents, locate witnesses, and take statements from them. Barristers, who are engaged by solicitors, are the ones who appear in court and actually try cases.

The analogy is not exact, because the solicitor retains the barrister of his choice, whereas the American lawyer is the supervisor and employer of the paralegal, who cannot give legal advice or represent a client in court. Solicitors give legal advice and perform many of the same legal tasks that American lawyers perform, such as drawing up wills and handling probate matters, without the supervision of a barrister. The barrister is in charge only in trial matters. Despite these differences, the role of the paralegal under our system is at least approximate to that of the British solicitor.

The NFPA's previously quoted statement that "the tasks and responsibilities of paralegals vary depending upon the areas of law and the level of experience of the individual paralegal" deserves some expansion. Many law firms hire paralegals as specialists in a single field, and accordingly many schools offer specialized courses. Thus a paralegal may be a specialist in probate, real estate, corporate law, litigation, or any number of other specialized areas, and work only on cases within that field. On the other hand, he may be hired as a general paralegal and work on any case that comes into the office.

"The level of experience of the individual paralegal" is another large variable. Many paralegals, particularly in public agencies such as courts or district attorneys' offices, are in-house trained, and have no formal education at all in the field. And because there are no general standards for paralegals, the training of those who do have schooling varies tremendously. Law courses are more or less standard across the nation, so that the graduate of virtually any law school is equipped, at least theoretically, to pass the bar examination of any state. But paralegal courses vary all the way from one nine-week summer course to four years of full-time courses leading to a bachelor's degree. One school even offers a master's degree in paralegal studies, requiring a year and a half of study beyond a bachelor's degree.

A graduate of any of these courses can call himself a paralegal, and can usually show a certificate to prove it. But obviously the pay and responsibilities of a nineteen-year-old graduate of a six-month night-school course are not going to be the same as those offered to a paralegal holding a bachelor's degree. Both may be given the title of "paralegal," but the former's duties, at least to start, are likely to be closer to those of an office clerk, and the salary is likely to be on the level of a clerk also. The latter will probably start right out doing legal work at a substantially higher salary.

Some experienced and trusted paralegals are for all practical purposes practicing law, although every paralegal I talked to was extremely careful to stay within state law and abide by the rules of the ABA concerning the unauthorized practice of law.

Los Angeles attorney Charles Rosenberg, who is also an instructor in the UCLA Attorney Assistant Training Program, wrote in an article in the *Los Angeles Lawyer* for July 1978:

> Most things that lawyers do can be done by people who didn't go to law school—and be done quite well at that.... When a lawyer first gives a research assignment (or any other sort of assignment) to a paralegal whose abilities in that area are previously unknown to the lawyer, the lawyer has a heavy responsibility to check the work until reasonably satisfied that it has been properly done. As experience with a particular paralegal... advances, such close checking becomes less necessary.

This, I discovered in talking with dozens of paralegals, is a common development. As the supervising lawyer of a paralegal who consistently turns out flawless work gains more and more trust in the paralegal, his checking of the work tends to become more and more cursory. Every paralegal I talked to who had that kind of relationship with his employer claimed to go to considerable lengths not to take advantage of it, however. Every one felt that it was ethically necessary to keep the lawyer with whom he worked informed of even the most minute detail of his work. All briefs, all letters, all documents of any kind prepared by the paralegal therefore went across the supervising lawyer's desk. A number of paralegals candidly admitted to me that they doubted that everything was read before being signed or initialed, but they felt that was the lawyer's responsibility, and that they had discharged their responsibility by presenting the material for checking.

They felt this protected the interests of both the paralegal and the attorney. The attorney's signature or initials on each item constitutes documentary evidence that everything the paralegal has done was under a lawyer's supervision, and thus he not only avoids the appearance of practicing law without a license, but cannot be held accountable by the client for any mistakes. (As previously cited from Opinion 316 of the ABA Standing Committee on Ethics and Professional Responsibility, the lawyer is solely responsible to the client for all work done under his supervision.) As for the lawyer, it is only fair that he at least have the opportunity to check everything done in his name, since he is the accountable one.

Paralegal work sometimes involves travel. Melissa Sugar, who works in the legal department at Shell Oil Company's Houston headquarters, has been sent to both coasts by her company. The first trip, in 1976, was taken because Shell had just begun to hire paralegals (Melissa was the second ever hired) and wasn't quite sure just how to use them. The head of her department sent Melissa and a co-worker to Washington, D.C., for the purpose of observing how paralegals were being used by a major law firm in the nation's capital. As a result of this study, many new areas were opened up for paralegals at Shell, where formerly they had been used primarily for mere clerical duties.

Her other trip was to Los Angeles, where she was sent

for a week to search documents in connection with a subpoena.

A paralegal in the antitrust department of one of Atlanta's largest law firms has at various times been sent by her firm to Pennsylvania, Ohio, and Alabama to investigate documents related to her cases.

Paralegals are sometimes even sent out of the country. One New York City paralegal, who works for a maritime firm, traveled to Hong Kong as part of a legal team that represented her firm in a multimillion-dollar ship purchase.

On the whole most paralegals find their work quite interesting, with occasional dramatic high points. But there is also a considerable amount of dull routine work that must be done. It is not all dull, but you should not expect that entering the field will give you the opportunity to live the dramatic life of a Perry Mason, or his Girl Friday, Della Street.

2

Paralegals in Action

The taxi trip from Manhattan to John F. Kennedy Airport took an hour and a half because of heavy traffic, getting Jim (who requested that his last name not be used) there only ten minutes before his flight time. He hurried into the terminal, carrying his single small suitcase, and trotted over to the flight-schedule board.

Flight 101 from New York City to Athens, Greece, was posted as canceled.

Oh, fine, thought Jim. Maybe I'll have to swim.

He went to the reservation desk and asked the clerk, "How long will the flight to Athens be delayed?"

"It's not a delay; it's a cancellation," the clerk told him. "The plane has been taken out of service because of mechanical problems."

"Okay, when's the next flight?"

"A week from today."

"A week!" Jim repeated in a slightly high voice. "I have to be back in a week."

"Sorry," the clerk said politely. "I could get you on a flight to Rome."

Jim examined him with mild exasperation. "My business happens to be in Athens."

"Well, Rome is considerably closer to Athens than New York City. And Olympic Airways runs a shuttle flight from there to Athens."

"All right," Jim said. "Get me a reservation on the shuttle flight."

"I can't do that. They accept only personally made reservations. You'll have to make your own arrangements after you arrive in Rome."

"How soon can you get me on a plane to Rome?" Jim asked resignedly.

"A flight leaves in one hour."

"Put me on it," Jim said.

If he was unable to get a flight from Rome to Athens, he was going to be in big trouble, Jim thought as he winged his way toward Rome. It was now Saturday, May 15, 1976. He estimated it would take him at least three days to dig up all the information he needed in Athens. And he had to be back in New York City when court opened at 9 A.M. on Monday, May 24.

Jim was being sent to Athens by his law firm to make a document search in connection with an admiralty case involving three different countries. The plaintiff and the defendant were both Greek ship owners. A London insurance company was the defendant's insurer, and the case was being tried in a United States District Court.

In 1974 two Greek-owned freighters collided in a

dense fog within the territorial waters of the United States. One sank; the other was sufficiently damaged to be laid up for repairs for sixty days.

The owner of the damaged ship felt that blame for the accident was equally divided between the two captains, and that therefore the cost of the damage should be equally divided. As the other ship was a total loss, and the owner of the damaged ship was offering to assume responsibility for half the damage to both ships, he felt he was making a generous offer. However, the owner of the sunken ship brought suit to make the other owner pay 100 percent of the damages.

The damaged ship was insured by a London insurance company, and the insurers had retained Jim's New York City law firm to defend the action.

As part of the defense it was necessary to show the precise monetary loss to the defendant because of the accident. This included not only the cost of repairs, but the loss in revenue during the sixty days the ship was in dry dock being repaired. In order to compute that, the legal firm asked the ship owner to submit all shipping contracts, bills of lading, and cargo invoices for the periods sixty days prior to the collision and sixty days after the ship was placed back in service.

The case was scheduled to go to trial on May 24, 1976. Despite repeated letters and transatlantic phone calls by the defense lawyers to the defendant in Greece, the requested material didn't arrive until ten days before the trial. And only about half the necessary documents had been sent.

In view of the delay in getting any action out of the defendant, the defense team felt it would be dangerous to try to prod the rest of the documents out of the defendant by long distance. It was decided to send a member of the law firm to Greece to pick them up.

Jim was chosen. He was not one of the fifty lawyers in the firm, but one of its eight paralegals. This choice was made, not because the assignment was too unimportant for a lawyer to undertake, but because Jim was better equipped for the job than any of the firm's junior lawyers. Through experience and training paralegals often become more knowledgeable in specialized areas than even the senior members of their firms, and Jim happened to be an expert in document searches.

When he landed in Rome, Jim headed for the Olympic Airways reservation desk even before collecting his baggage. The earliest flight to Athens was Tuesday afternoon. The reservation clerk suggested he arrive early, as they routinely overbooked, and passengers were accepted on a first come-first-served basis.

With no choice but to wait for Tuesday to arrive, Jim decided to relax and enjoy himself. On Sunday and Monday he toured Rome. Tuesday morning he arrived at the airport four hours before flight time in order to ensure himself a seat. While waiting for his flight to be called, he phoned Athens to report when he would be flying in.

At the Athens airport he was met by an English-speaking guide from the shipping company. He was driven directly to the company office; then his luggage was sent on to a hotel where a reservation had been made for him.

With the help of company clerks, Jim began his document search that evening. Working night and day, he managed to glean everything he needed from the files and get all the documents photocopied by Thursday night. As his return flight was scheduled for Saturday, that gave him one day to take in the sights of Athens.

He arrived back in New York City late Sunday night and delivered his documents to the courtroom on Monday morning just in time for the opening of the trial. The documents proved to be of major importance to the case. The decision of the court was to affix damages equally between the plaintiff and the defendant.

The work paralegals do is seldom as glamorous as this particular case. Jim, for instance, cannot recall what cases he worked on during the two months immediately following this admiralty case, which indicates they couldn't have been very exciting. Dramatic cases are few and far between, he says, and most of a paralegal's work is routine.

Doris Peckner, on the other hand, says that *all* of her cases are interesting. A trim, attractive woman, Doris works directly under Attorney Stanley K. Jacobs in the Century City, California, law office of Memel, Jacobs, Pierno and Gersh. Since Stan Jacobs specializes in personal-injury claims, naturally that is Doris Peckner's specialty also.

Doris recalls a case that she won for her firm in seven minutes. That is how long she had been researching the law on the matter when she discovered a precedent that won the case.

The case involved an injury that resulted in the paralysis of an eight-year-old boy who had been riding a dirt bike that crashed into another motorcycle rider. The investigation virtually cleared the other motorcyclist of any responsibility for the accident. In addition, he was uninsured, so suing him for damages would have been pointless. On the other hand, the injured boy's mother did not have an insurance policy that provided coverage for injuries caused by the negligent use, ownership, or maintenance of a dirt bike.

However, the mother carried a homeowner's policy that covered her for liability for general negligent acts, unrelated to motor vehicles, both at home and away from home. The parents of the boy were divorced, and the boy lived with his mother. The father brought suit against the mother on behalf of the boy for compensatory damages, charging her with negligence in allowing an eight-year-old to ride a dirt bike without proper supervision.

Although the boy's injuries were worth considerably more, damages of $100,000 were asked because that was the limit of coverage on the homeowner's policy.

The insurance company refused to pay on the grounds that the policy contained a clause specifically exempting it from liability for accidents involving motor vehicles.

Doris Peckner was assigned the task of researching the law on the matter. She had been poring over similar cases in the law firm's library for exactly seven minutes when she found the crucial precedent.

In another case involving the negligent use of a motor vehicle and a separate act of negligence by the same wrongdoer that combined to cause serious injury, a trial court found that both the automobile insurer and the homeowner insurance carrier were required to pay damages. Although the Court of Appeal held in that case that only the automobile policy was applicable, the California Supreme Court had reversed the decision of the Court of Appeal and declared that payment for damages had to be made by both the automobile and the homeowner carriers, on the theory that the use of the vehicle was only one of the causes of the injuries. That is, since two separate acts of negligence caused the accident, both the automobile policy and the homeowner's policy provided coverage.

When this decision was shown to the boy's mother's insurance company, it instantly agreed to make full payment. The reason for its capitulation was a previous court decision that left it open to damages even greater than the policy limit if it refused settlement. In that case, the plaintiff had offered to accept a certain settlement, but the offer was rejected by the insurance company. The plaintiff had then brought suit for a much larger amount—one in excess of the insurance coverage—and had won the case. The court held that because the insurance company had rejected the original offer to settle, thus eventually costing the client more than the amount of his insurance coverage, it was now liable to pay the full award. In view of this precedent, the company carrying the boy's mother's homeowner's policy had no desire to allow the matter to proceed to trial, where it could be held liable for the entire verdict, because it had not settled the case within the $100,000 coverage when it had opportunity to do so.

Doris Peckner emphasizes that while she finds all her cases interesting, that doesn't mean that every minute of every working day is fraught with drama. There are frequent thrills in the work, such as the discovery of the precedent that won what she has come to call her "seven-minute case," but a good deal of time is spent on routine, sometimes dull matters.

For example, during the two weeks prior to the time I interviewed her, Doris had scheduled twenty-two depositions, which had to be coordinated with five other law firms, had arranged for the serving of two dozen subpoenas (some of which she served herself, when they were friendly witnesses, in order to save clients the service fees), and had pored through dozens of law books in researching the law involved in various cases. None of this work was very exciting in itself, but she regarded each case she worked on as an exciting challenge. Doris feels that the sense of accomplishment experienced from the successful handling of a case is compensation for the hard, sometimes burdensome work that goes into it.

A paralegal for a large Midwestern law firm told me the following story, but asked that neither her name nor her firm be revealed.

The paralegal, whom we will call Mary, works for a firm that has sixty lawyers and ten paralegals. The latter are all specialists. One handles nothing but probate; two are specialists in corporate law; one is a real-estate expert; and the other six specialize in litigation. Mary is one of the litigation specialists.

At her firm the litigation paralegals rotate the chore of doing initial interviews of new clients who come in off the street. Mary was on duty the day an enormously fat woman weighing well over three hundred pounds entered her office. Introducing herself as Miss Angela Speck (not her real name), the woman asked if Mary handled lawsuits.

"The firm does," Mary told her. "I am not a lawyer, but a legal assistant . If we take your case, it will be assigned to one of our lawyers. I may assist him, but he will be in charge of the case."

"I see," Miss Speck said. "Well, I want to sue a doctor."

"On what grounds?"

"He treated me for eight months to lose weight."

"And you didn't lose any?"

"Oh, I lost weight all right," Angela Speck said. "Nigh onto fifty pounds. But at the end of eight months I gave

31

birth to a baby." She added extraneously, "I ain't married, but I know who the father is."

Mary stared at her. "The doctor wasn't aware that you were pregnant?"

The woman shook her head.

"Why didn't you tell him?"

"Because I didn't know either."

Mary stared some more. Finally she said, "You mean to say you had no idea you were pregnant until you gave birth?"

"That's right. I think he should have given me some kind of test and told me."

"Weren't there any symptoms?" Mary asked, fascinated. "I mean, you must have noticed you were no longer menstruating."

"I thought maybe I was in change of life."

"Didn't you have any morning sickness, or ever feel the baby kick?"

"Oh he kicked some toward the end, but I thought it was indigestion."

Mary was silent for a time, in a state of partial shock, as she tried to imagine how any woman, even one as overweight as Angela Speck, could carry a baby for a full nine months without realizing she was pregnant. Finally she asked, "Was it a normal birth?"

The woman shook her head again. "He ain't right. The doctor I got now says he never will be. He also says the reducing pills the other doctor give me could of caused it."

"Then it seems you may have grounds for suit," Mary said, pulling her note pad in front of her. "I am not allowed to decide that, because I am not a lawyer. I will pass on the information to my supervisor, however, and he will let you know whether or not the firm will take your case. Let's start by your giving me the names of both doctors."

The case was taken by her firm, and though this remains one of Mary's favorite cases, it wasn't a successful one, despite being a virtually made-to-order malpractice suit. It developed that the doctor was so incompetent that quite a few of his former patients were suing him for malpractice. In self-defense the doctor disappeared. Eventually it was learned that he had fled to Europe, but Mary could never locate him. Angela Speck never recovered damages, therefore, but the suit remains on file, and if the good doctor ever resurfaces, she still has a chance to recover.

Phyllis Cardoza, an affable, efficient-looking brunette, is an independent paralegal who works out of her own office in Westwood, an exclusive section of Los Angeles, for some thirty different lawyers. Her specialty is probate, and she is kept busy because she knows more about it than most lawyers. Generally she has about eighty cases running at any one time.

Phyllis got into paralegal work by accident. She had been a legal secretary, but she resigned her job to have a baby. She had planned to stay home and care for the child until it was at least three years old, but her former boss contacted her and asked her to handle a probate case at home. She handled it so well that he gave her more cases. Word spread among other law firms, and eventually she was getting enough work to justify renting her own office and hiring her own secretary.

Phyllis credits her rather exceptional success to her specialized knowledge. Few lawyers specialize in probate, she says, and unless they do, they usually do not know a

33

great deal about it. A litigation specialist or a corporation lawyer, for example, will get some probate business because he has drawn up wills for clients who initially came to him for other reasons, or a relative of some client dies and the client asks him to handle the estate. But since probate is essentially a sideline, a lawyer is likely to be rusty on it. Rather than do a lot of brushing up on the subject, and incidentally be sidetracked from more important business, he will engage Phyllis to handle the matter.

Like all paralegals, she sends all the documents she draws up and all correspondence across the desk of the lawyer she is working for, but her expertise is held in such esteem that approval is usually routine. Even when some unusual situation requires an action unfamiliar to the supervising attorney, it is seldom questioned because the lawyer is confident that she has thoroughly researched the matter and that the action is the correct one.

Phyllis Cardoza's initial training was all in-house as a legal secretary. She actually had no formal paralegal training until she was in business as an independent paralegal. During the eight years she has been in business for herself she has acquired considerable formal training, though. In addition to taking courses designed for both paralegals and attorneys specializing in probate and tax matters at a number of different schools, she has also taken courses in the techniques of legal research and has attended numerous bar-association seminars.

One of Phyllis' favorite cases happens to be one of the first she handled as an independent. It was a case inherited by her former boss through a rather complicated set of circumstances, and one he felt little obligation to handle personally because the deceased had not been his client.

The case involved the estate of Everett Manners (not the real name), who had died nearly nine years previously. Unfortunately, the lawyer handling the probate died shortly after Manners, and before filing for probate. Everett Manners had a brother and two sisters, but he had not been in contact with them for many years, and they were unaware of his death. Since he had died intestate, and they were his closest living relatives, they were each entitled to a third of his estate. But, being unaware that they were heirs, naturally they had made no inquiries.

The case lay among the deceased lawyer's papers for eight years before it was discovered. It was immediatly assigned to another lawyer in the firm, but soon after that he left the firm to go into partnership with Phyllis' boss. He took the case with him, which now made it the responsibility of the new partnership.

Before getting around to doing anything about the case, the new partner was named to a vacated judgeship by the governor of California, and all his pending cases were turned over to Phyllis' boss. Phyllis had quit to have her baby only a short time before all this. Her ex-boss called on her to straighten out the probate case he had inherited.

The case itself was not very complicated. It consisted primarily of a house valued at about thirty thousand dollars and some money for its rental in an escrow account. Although the original lawyer handling the estate hadn't filed any probate papers before he died, he had gotten around to arranging with a realty company to handle the house's rental.

The first thing Phyllis had to do was locate the heirs. When she had done that, she filed the necessary opening papers, informed the heirs of the hearing to appoint an administrator, then proceeded with the inventory of the estate and the determination of inheritance taxes. All this had to be done before the house could be sold.

The brother and two sisters of the deceased, all quite elderly, lived in separate communities, but all within a fifty-mile radius of Los Angeles. From the moment they discovered they were in for some money, their concern over their long-dead brother, whom none had bothered to inquire about during the past twenty years, became immense. The sisters wanted to know all the details of his death, and incidentally to know the size of the estate and how soon it would be settled. The surviving brother, who lived in Upland, California, about thirty-five miles from Los Angeles, was interested only in the latter. Although he had made no attempt to contact his brother in two decades, he phoned Phyllis weekly, now that the man was dead, to inquire when his money would be forthcoming.

There was some delay on that because the estate couldn't be settled until the house was sold. Phyllis managed to find a buyer almost immediately, but the buyer applied for a Federal Housing Authority loan, and the FHA required that a number of repairs be made to the house before it would approve the loan. But eventually the sale was consummated, court approval was obtained, the estate was closed, and checks went out to the three heirs.

Enclosed with each check was a receipt to be signed by the recipient. The receipts from the two sisters came in promptly, but the one from the brother never arrived, although his canceled check came back, stamped as cashed the day after it was mailed. Phyllis wrote him a couple of letters, to which she received no replies, and finally she telephoned Upland. The man's wife answered the phone.

"Your husband hasn't returned his receipt," Phyllis told her. "I need it to file with the probate court."

"He can't sign it," the wife said.

"Why not?" Phyllis asked, surprised. "He signed the check."

"That's because he took it right down to the bank to deposit it in our joint account. He was going to sign the receipt as soon as he got home, but just as he walked in the door, he dropped dead."

Remembering the weekly phone calls she had received from the man, Phyllis couldn't help thinking that there was wry justice in his never getting to benefit from the money he had been so eager to receive from a dead brother whom he had never bothered about while he was alive.

Linda Glasgow, an attractive paralegal in her twenties, is office manager for the Century City law firm of Bollington, Pennell, Stilz and Bloeser. Prior to her present job, which she began in early 1979, she was a litigation paralegal for the Los Angeles firm of Olney, Levy and Kaplan.

Linda finds office management just as interesting as her former paralegal work, and somewhat more prestigious. Though she is now involved in such matters as paying and collecting bills, hiring and firing office staff, and figuring profits for tax purposes, rather than in legal matters, she finds her paralegal background of vital importance in running a law office.

"There are problems unique to a law office that are not found in the ordinary business office," she says. "And a paralegal background is invaluable in solving them."

Considering that she is only in her twenties, Linda holds an important job. It is not one for which there are many openings, however. Obviously there can never be as many openings for law office managers as there are for other paralegals, simply because there is but one office manager to an office, whereas there may be a dozen or more paralegals. Nevertheless, it is a growing field for those more interested in administration than in law.

Maryann Altman, of Altman and Wells, a legal consulting firm in Philadelphia, says she is often asked by law firms to find administrators. "It is a relatively new field and growth has been dramatic," she says. She cautions, however, that opportunities are rare unless applicants have both considerable legal office experience and an administrative background.

Recognizing that there is at least some demand for administrators in the legal profession, a number of schools offering paralegal training offer optional courses in legal administration. These include such subjects as employee benefits, commercial transactions, accounting, legal technology, budget and financial planning, law library administration, and computer operation.

Though openings for administrators are limited, those who do manage to squeeze into the field are likely to find the pay better than that of paralegals working in legal jobs. Eighteen to twenty thousand a year is not uncommon for office managers, and salaries at the bigger firms in large metropolitan areas have been known to run as high as forty-five thousand a year.

3

Where Paralegals Find Jobs

The most recent study of the subject by the ABA's Standing Committee on Legal Assistants is titled *Legal Assistant Education and Utilization: a 1978 Status Report,* and runs eighty-one pages. Part of the study involved a survey of the graduates of 150 different schools offering paralegal training to determine what specialty courses they had taken, within what legal fields they had found employment, and what types of employers had hired them. A total of 4,169 graduates of 1977 were included in the survey.

Most of the schools examined in the study used a generalized approach in which they attempted to prepare students for positions where they would be expected to perform a variety of legal tasks. But programs of short duration, particularly those accepting primarily college graduates, tended to gear their programs toward training specialists. These programs usually devoted their entire three-to-four-month courses to developing expertise in only one field of legal practice.

The 150 surveyed schools reported the following specialties offered, listed in order of popularity. The number of schools out of the 150 offering each specialty is also listed:

Specialty Course	*Number of Schools Offering It*
Estate Planning and Probate	108
Litigation	94
Real Estate or Property Law	94
Business Organization or Corporate Law	78
Family or Domestic Law	73
Criminal Law	40
Law Office Management	38
Income Taxation and Accounting	28
Insurance and Torts	21
Bankruptcy	16
Administrative Law	13
Contracts	13

According to the survey results, there was a good correlation between the types of work the graduates were doing and the emphasis given to those fields in the educational programs. These are the fields in which the graduates were specializing:

Legal Area	Percentage Employed
Litigation	25
Estates and Trusts	20
Real Estate	19
Business Organization or Corporate Law	15
Domestic or Family Law	8.5
General Practice	6
Criminal Law	5
Income Taxation	1.5

Large law firms (classified for purposes of the survey as those with more than fifteen lawyers) proved to be the largest employers of the graduates, with 27.3 percent of all placements. Law firms of all sizes provided the majority of jobs, employing 56.4 percent of the graduates. Here is the reported employment of graduates by employer category:

Employer	Number Employed	Percentage Employed
Large law firm (more than 15 lawyers)	1,136	27.3
Small law firm (less than 6 lawyers)	631	15.2
Medium-sized law firm (6 to 15 lawyers)	581	13.9
Government or other community service agencies	302	7.2
Corporate legal departments	272	6.5
Non-law-related positions	246	5.9

Employer	Number Employed	Percentage Employed
Insurance companies, banks, or other financial institutions	243	5.8
Other law-related positions	201	4.8
Unemployed or information not available	557	13.4
TOTAL	4,169	100

The statistic that 13.4 percent of the graduates were either unemployed or that information about them was unavailable is somewhat misleading. Directors of the reporting schools noted that many of the unemployed were that way by choice, because they had chosen to go on to law school, continue their education in some other field, or for other reasons had not sought jobs following graduation. Furthermore, at least some of those about whom no information was available (because they failed to answer questionnaires) probably had jobs.

Although the ABA, with typical lawyer's caution, made no such guess, it seems reasonable to assume from the statistics that at least 95 percent of the 1977 graduates who wanted jobs found them.

This is substantiated on a local level by a survey made by Southern Career Institute of Boca Raton, Florida, which found that 94 percent of its graduates were working in the legal community. Its other findings were close to those of the ABA survey also. Southern Career found that 60 percent of its working graduates worked in law offices (compared to the ABA figure of 56.3 nationally); the other 34 percent had jobs involving legal work for governmental agencies, community organizations, and businesses other than law firms.

Both of these surveys involved only formally trained paralegals, of course. There are thousands of paralegals, particularly in governmental agencies on all levels, who have never been surveyed because they were in-house trained and the surveyors are generally unaware of their existence. For example, I talked to a man who had worked as a paralegal for the Ventura County, California, District Attorney's Office for seven years, yet had no formal legal training whatever. He was a career Navy man, who for a time had an assignment that involved the administration of military law; on the basis of that experience, he got his job as a paralegal after retirement.

Many such paralegals were hired without formal training simply because the need exceeded the number of available graduates. But that situation has so drastically changed that the chance of landing a paralegal job without either formal training or experience (as a legal secretary, for example) is rapidly sinking to zero. In 1970 there were only five schools in the country offering paralegal training. By 1976 the number had jumped to 125. In 1979 it had reached 257.

The Los Angeles Paralegal Association has 300 members, and estimates that there are about 300 more non-members working as paralegals in the Greater Los Angeles area. There have been approximately 1,000 graduates of the various schools in the area to date, which is 400 more than have local jobs. That doesn't mean that 400 paralegals are looking for work in Los Angeles, because many of the students came from other areas to take their training, and returned to their home towns on graduation. But it does mean that an untrained and inexperienced job applicant is competing with an adequate supply of trained paralegals.

In the past many employers were willing to invest the

time and money for the in-house training of applicants who struck them as intelligent enough to learn the work, but that is no longer necessary. Now that trained personnel are available, more and more employers simply refuse to bother with in-house training programs, regardless of how appealing untrained and inexperienced applicants may be.

The list of employers other than law firms using the services of paralegals is growing so fast that the point may soon be reached where they are the major employers rather than law firms. In the public sector, on the federal level, paralegals are employed by the Justice Department, the Internal Revenue Service, the Department of Health, Education and Welfare, and some two dozen other departments, bureaus, and administrative agencies. On the state level they find work in even greater numbers. On the local level they are hired by the offices of public defenders, district attorneys, city and county managers, police departments, sheriff's departments, legal aid societies, court-reporting agencies, bail-bonding companies, and a host of other agencies and organizations.

In the private sector the variety of jobs available is growing just as fast. In Chapter 1 a paralegal employed by the Shell Oil Company was mentioned. All large corporations have legal departments, and more and more are discovering that they can save money, without lowering the quality of work done in such departments, by hiring paralegals to free lawyers from routine duties so that their time can be more usefully spent on matters that only lawyers should handle.

The present primary source of employment for paralegals—private law firms—has hardly been tapped. Although one San Diego law firm claims to have employed a paralegal as early as 1948, it is less than a decade since paralegals began to be used in any appreciable numbers. New ideas always encounter resistance, and the legal profession tends to be particularly conservative. Thousands of lawyers, pariculary the older ones, have so far refused to accept the whole idea of paralegals.

Lawyers don't necessarily have to be old to be hidebound conservatives. One lawyer I talked to expressed the opinion that the paralegal profession was both over-rated and overblown. "I would much rather have a good legal secretary," he told me. "A really good secretary can do anything a paralegal can, and type too."

The speaker was not an old fogey from a large law firm, but a man in his thirties in a two-man law firm whose only other employee was a legal secretary.

There is a feeling both among the directors of paralegal associations and the directors of schools offering paralegal training that converting such reactionaries to the acceptance of the paralegal profession will open up many more employment opportunities. To that end, both groups carry on educational campaigns directed at the legal profession in attempts to convince lawyers of the advantages of hiring paralegals.

In its brochure *The Legal Assistant*, the University of West Los Angeles, the first school in southern California to receive ABA approval, makes this blunt statement:

The legal profession is plagued with more serious problems that it cares to admit. Consumer groups and governmental agencies are calling for an increase in the quality, effectiveness and availability of legal services while challenging rising legal costs. The efficiency of the profession is being questioned by proponents of group legal services and no-fault insurance while others have attacked fee schedules. Corporations and other businesses are seeking methods to reduce the costs of legal services. Furthermore, while the cost of legal services is rising, surveys indicate that real income to the attorney is falling.

If attorneys wish to preserve their well-deserved stature in society, they must respond to this wave of criticism. Of the many solutions and improvements that have been suggested, the one which has been universally accepted by the organized bar is the use of the legal paraprofessional. The proper utilization of a well-trained legal assistant is one of the most effective means of meeting the needs of business and the public and their demands to cut rising legal costs.

At another point in the brochure this argument for the employment of paralegals is directed at attorneys:

If you or your associates find yourselves in any of the following situations, you need a paralegal—whether part-time, full-time, free-lance or temporary:

1. Swamped with routine paperwork.
2. Handling research, procedural or drafting matters that do not require the use of attorney skills.
3. Turning away matters because of lack of time.
4. Feeling the maximum effort has not been devoted to a matter.
5. Reducing billing to a client because the time spent on the matter was not warranted.
6. Taking routine telephone calls concerning simple matters such as the status of a case.
7. Experiencing a decrease in income.

46

Spring Hill College of Mobile, Alabama, mails this flier to local attorneys in an attempt to induce them to hire the college's graduates:

FOUR REASONS FOR HIRING A LEGAL ASSISTANT

I. *A Legal Assistant Can Increase Income*
    a. Can free a lawyer's time to do those tasks *only* a lawyer can do, i.e.
        1. Give legal advice
        2. Attend and participate in trials
        3. Take depositions
    b. As a result of freeing the lawyer's time, you have
        1. More *attorney* billable hours
        2. Legal assistant billable hours

II. *A Legal Assistant Can Increase Caseload/Clientele*
    a. Lawyer has more time for lawyering
    b. Lawyer has more time for those activities that *lead* to increased clientele
        1. Social
        2. Community
        3. Church
        4. Political
        5. Professional

III. *A Legal Assistant Can Increase Lawyer-Client Contact and Improve That Relationship*
    a. Lawyer and legal assistant work together as a team
        1. Introduce legal assistant at *first* client contact
        2. Doubles the number of people aware of case posture, activities, and needs

47

      b. Legal assistant can handle the preponderance of client contacts, further freeing the lawyer to do lawyer-only work

      c. Client is more satisfied with handling of the case

         1. May recommend attorney to friends

         2. Despite eventual outcome, is less likely to have a bad feeling regarding information flow to him

         3. Client may save money

IV. *A Legal Assistant Can Decrease Office Errors*

      a. Systematic approach to substantive areas of law minimizes chance of missed documents or filing time problems

      b. Much less likelihood of ever being on the wrong end of a malpractice suit

      c. Fewer errors mean more billable time

As the brochure of the University of West Los Angeles indicates, the use of the legal paraprofessional has been pretty much accepted by "the organized bar" (the ABA and various state and local bar associations). It is fairly evident that there has been such acceptance because many training programs are actively sponsored by bar associations, and in many cases were formed at the suggestion of bar associations.

Such associations do not speak for all of their individual members, though, and it is obvious that some of those members are either opposed or indifferent to the use of paralegals. There is more and more acceptance all the time, however, and perhaps the educational efforts of paralegal associations and schools will eventually gain full acceptance.

At least the situation is considerably improved over what it was in the infancy of the profession. A pioneer in the profession, a Los Angeles grandmother who made the in-house transition from legal secretary to paralegal fifteen years ago, long before any schools in the area began teaching legal assistance, describes the problems she faced in those days.

"I felt like an outcast for three years or so," she says. "I didn't belong to any group in the office. At first the older attorneys resisted. They were always gentlemanly, but they felt because I didn't have a law degree and was a woman and had been a secretary, I should stay a secretary. Then other secretaries didn't see why I should have any perquisites or why I should make more money. And the younger attorneys were eager to do my work themselves."

With the moral support of her immediate superior, who happened to be one of the senior lawyers in the firm and who was the one who had promoted her to paralegal status, she managed to weather the storm. Her performance was a major factor in her victory. Gradually, she says, she won acceptance from all sides just by doing a competent job. Her law firm, which has thirty lawyers, now employs eight paralegals.

An even more encouraging indication is the findings of an in-house survey made in 1978 by one of New Orleans' major law firms, which currently has twenty-nine lawyers and six paralegals on its staff. One of the projections was to prophesy what the size of the firm would be in twenty years. It was forecast that by 1998 it would employ sixty lawyers and sixty paralegals.

If it eventually becomes a national trend to have law firms consisting of as many paralegals as lawyers, the opportunities for employment of trained paralegals will expand enormously.

49

4

Pros and Cons

The most irritating question a prospective employer can ask an applicant for a paralegal job is, "Can you type?"

Paralegal Linda Glasgow charges that this is a sexist question because it is asked only of female applicants. My interviews of paralegals bore this out. I encountered a number of female paralegals who had been asked this question, but no male paralegals who had ever been.

The fact that ability to type is an advantage in any profession, including the practice of law, is beside the point. The question suggests a rather widespread misunderstanding among lawyers as to just what paralegals are supposed to do. In the last chapter the resistance of some lawyers to the use of paralegals in any capacity was discussed. Although that prejudice is gradually being overcome, it is nearly as frustrating to paralegals to discover

50

that acceptance doesn't necessarily include understanding.

Linda Glasgow points out that no senior member of a
law firm interviewing a newly admitted member of the
bar whom the firm was considering offering a position
would dream of asking if the applicant could type, regardless of sex. The question to a paralegal suggests that
the prospective employer's mental image of paralegals,
particularly if they are female, is that they are some kind
of exalted clerk.

Of course in many law firms where paralegals have
been employed for some time, each person's particular
skills are fully utilized. None of the paralegals described
in Chapter 2 were treated as clerks by their employers.
But as a general rule, in firms where paralegals are just
beginning to be employed, there is, at least initially, considerable confusion on the part of the firms' lawyers as to
just what the roles of the new employees should be.

This situation is also likely to exist in corporate institutions other than law firms. The incident described in
Chapter 1, in which a pair of paralegals employed by the
Shell Oil Company was sent to Washington, D.C., to find
out just what paralegals were supposed to do, was unusual only in the action taken. The confusion among
employers is quite common. Often there is a considerable
amount of floundering, both by employers and paralegals, when paralegals are first hired by a company as a
new experiment.

In a 1978 survey by the East Bay Association of Legal
Assistants, a group in Oakland, California, one respondent, a newly employed paralegal, commented queru-
lously: "Would like to know more precisely just what a
legal assistant is or does. No one seems to know, and at the

moment the type of work you receive depends entirely on the attorney who gives it."

Another respondent complained: " . . . the trend seems to be using paralegals as typists, i.e. 'paralegal pools.' I feel this will discourage high-caliber people from staying in the field."

The uncertainty of how you are going to be treated on your first paralegal job is an obvious drawback to the profession. You *may* be treated as the professional you are from the moment you begin your first job, of course. But there is equal likelihood that you will not be.

Most of the paralegals I talked to who worked for large law firms felt that the proper function of the paralegal was both understood and respected by the lawyers of their firms. One woman paralegal mentioned that this was shown not only in the type of work and responsibilities delegated to her and her paralegal colleagues, but also in more subtle manifestations of acceptance, such as the acceptance of the firm's paralegals in social events once limited to lawyers. As an example, she cited a recent party to welcome a new lawyer joining the firm to which all the paralegals were invited along with the lawyers.

One of the respondents to the East Bay survey expressed a similar sentiment when she said: "More accepted as part of the legal profession. On occasion have gone into chambers in attorney's absence—was *not* treated hostilely by judge."

At least a fourth of the respondents had negative comments to make, though. Here are three selected at random: "There is still too much resistance to paralegals and too few areas of the law where paralegals can work." "I think we have a long way to go to being accepted as an established profession. Being a legal assistant means being in a no-man's land—floating somewhere between an attorney and a secretary in other people's minds, but with no defined position." "I do not feel that legal assisting has enough to offer at this point to consider itself a profession. A significant change in the attitude of attorneys will have to occur for this to come about. I, like many people, will most likely not be around that long."

That attitudes will change for the better (from the paralegals' point of view) as employers learn to use them more effectively is a probability. But as the last-quoted respondent to the East Bay survey wryly indicated, that may be a long time. Meantime, how you may expect to be treated as a brand-new paralegal employee seems to be a matter of chance. I made no extensive survey on the matter, but I got the impression from interviewing numerous paralegals that your best chance of finding a satisfactory professional relationship with your employer is in a large law firm that has employed paralegals for at least three years and has at least six on its staff.

Probably the greatest drawback to the paralegal profession is its nebulous standards. No doubt one reason for the confusion among attorneys about how to use paralegals is the confusion within the profession itself as to what the qualifications of a paralegal should be.

All fifty state legislatures have established standards for lawyers licensed to practice within their states, and all fifty state bar associations have set additional standards of practice and ethics. But no state legislature has passed any legislation concerning the qualifications or licensing of paralegals. The only state bar association attempting to set standards has been Oregon's, which certifies legal assistants. In order to obtain certification from the Oregon State Bar Association, the candidate must have an associate degree or an equivalent amount of college credit hours, must have completed forty-five credits in legal assistance courses, must have passed the certification examination given by the National Association of Legal Assistants, and must have two years of work experience in a legal environment.

How well has it worked?

The Career Information System of Eugene, Oregon, is a computer service that supplies schools with up-to-date information on career fields in Oregon. Terminals are placed in each school for students to use, and computer printouts may be obtained by punching in the proper codes. In early 1979, students received this printout when they punched the code for LEGAL ASSISTANTS:

CURRENT EMPLOYMENT: THIS IS A SMALL OCCUPATION WITH AROUND 150 PARALEGAL PERSONNEL EMPLOYED IN OREGON. ONE IS FORMALLY CERTIFIED.

In 1973 a bill was introduced in the California state legislature to establish a certification program for paralegals. It failed.

In 1977 there was a proposal for the California State Bar to establish a Certified Attorney Assistant Board with the authority to establish and control the certification and accreditation programs of paralegals, as well as the authority to discipline members of the profession. In November of 1978 the State Bar Board of Governors rejected the proposal.

The rejection was based on the recommendation of an ad hoc committee appointed to study the matter, which held public hearings in Los Angeles and San Francisco in the fall of 1977. The committee consisted of President

Nancy Siegel of the National Federation of Paralegal Associations and six attorneys.

The majority of testimony at both hearings was in opposition to the proposal. The NFPA, the East Bay Association of Legal Assistants, the Los Angeles Paralegal Association, the San Francisco Association of Legal Assistants, and numerous local paralegal associations from smaller communities were all strongly opposed. Among other opponents were the majority of schools offering paralegal training whose representatives testified, the Bar Association of San Francisco, the ABA Standing Committee on Legal Assistants, and many individual paralegals and lawyers.

Most of the opposition centered around the prematurity of certification and accreditation, the composition of the Certified Attorney Assistant Board, the possibly limiting effect certification could have on the development of the profession, the vagueness and lack of detail in the proposal, the possible negative effects certification could have on the delivery of legal services to the poor and elderly, and the question of the propriety of the State Bar controlling certification and accreditation.

It is possible that if there had been any generally recognized standards of education and performance by paralegals, the outcome would have been different. But the ad hoc committee was confronted with the problem of setting standards for a profession in which there was no uniformity of education, and in which duties ranged all the way from clerical to highly technical legal tasks. Under the circumstances the recommendation to reject the proposal seems wise.

A similar proposal for a certification program was defeated in Illinois. Florida, Kentucky, Maryland, and New

Mexico are considering certification programs, but so far have taken no positive action. Currently Kansas is the only state where a concerted effort is underway to establish a certification program, and that movement has pitted two paralegal associations against each other.

The Kansas Legal Assistants Society was formed in 1977 as a statewide organization for paralegals, and almost immediately petitioned the Kansas State Supreme Court for some form of certification for paralegals. The Supreme Court turned the matter over to the State Bar Association, which in mid-1978 appointed a Committee on Legal Assistants to study the matter. Wichita attorney John E. Foulston, who happens to be the employer of paralegal Karen Sanders-West, the president of KLAS, chairs the committee.

The Kansas City Association of Legal Assistants, whose membership covers the Greater Kansas City metropolitan area, has been in existence since 1975. Greater Kansas City is on the border between Missouri and Kansas and covers a four-county area in both states. About a third of KCALA's members either reside in or work in Kansas.

KCALA concurs with the opinion of the National Federation of Paralegal Associations that certification anywhere is premature until some national standards for paralegals have been developed by general custom and usage. The organization presented a paper to Mr. Foulston's committee and to the Kansas State Supreme Court entitled "Certification: Issues to be Considered." The gist of the paper was a protest that the committee had bypassed what KCALA considered a necessary first step—consideration of whether or not certification was appropriate at this time—and had jumped right into planning how to certify.

KLAS countered this move by presenting a position paper to the committee on November 1, 1978, stating that it "recommends and supports an examination and licensing program." It further recommended a comprehensive examination, even though some candidates may work in specialized areas of the law only. The paper said: "KLAS endorses a Kansas licensing examination which follows the guidelines of the Certified Legal Assistant Examination presently being conducted by the National Association of Legal Assistants, but KLAS recommends that a second test on Kansas Law be included."

As for requirements for the examination, KLAS recommended that a candidate be twenty-one years of age, work and live in Kansas, and (a) have completed a legal assistant program with at least sixty credit hours or have an associate degree with a minimum of twenty-six credit hours in law related courses, or (b) have a minimum of five years experience as a legal secretary *and* two years experience as a legal assistant *and* be endorsed by a practicing attorney.

To date the Kansas Bar Association has not acted on the proposal.

Eventually both state and nationwide standards for paralegals are virtually a certainty. It is the hope of most paralegal associations and of most schools offering paralegal training that they will be formed with caution, as it is much more difficult to amend or repeal unwise laws and regulations than it is to defeat them in the first place.

When nationwide standards do go into effect, what impact will they have on paralegals who are already working but fail to meet the set standards? Will in-house-trained paralegals or those with less formal education in legal assistance than required by the new rules automatically lose their jobs?

That seems unlikely. In the first place, employers will not be bound by the new rules, because Opinion 316 of the ABA Standing Committee on Ethics and Professional Responsibility (previously cited in Chapter 1) specifically permits lawyers to use any kind of lay assistants they please, so long as the assistants don't engage in the practice of law. In the second place, no employer is likely to release a satisfactory employee simply because of a bureaucratic ruling.

At worst, some employees calling themselves paralegals will have to stop using the term while continuing the same duties, but even that is unlikely. In the past when states began setting requirements for previously unregulated trades or professions, the tendency was to apply the new rules only to new candidates, and not disrupt the careers of those already practicing. For example, it was once possible to become a chiropractor after six months training. It is now a four-year course. No state has revoked the licenses of already practicing chiropractors since the new rules went into effect, however. In all probability, a similar provision will be made to allow already working paralegals to continue to call themselves paralegals regardless of whether or not they have the background decreed for licensing.

The most common complaint heard from paralegals is low salaries. It is true there are some horrible examples—in Schenectady, starting salaries range from $5200 to $6350 a year, and in parts of Michigan, Nebraska, and Texas they average less than $7000—but many experienced paralegals are well paid.

Debbie Korman, employment coordinator for the Los

Angeles Paralegal Association, reports that while starting salaries in the Los Angeles area run from a low of $10,000 to a high of $12,000, paralegals with as much as five years experience earn from $15,000 to $19,000. According to a 1978 survey by the San Francisco Association of Legal Assistants, the median salary for beginning paralegals was only $10,500 a year, but for those with six years experience it averaged $15,600, with a high of $28,800.

Debbie Korman has a pretty intimate knowledge of salary ranges in the Los Angeles area, and she reports the interesting phenomenon that paralegals are much more likely to receive salary increases by changing jobs than by simply waiting for raises. There is a rather tight market in the area for beginning paralegals, she says, but experienced paralegals are in demand. A paralegal with five or six years experience may walk into a law firm at a beginning salary of $16,000, even though paralegals with the same amount of experience in the same firm are receiving only $15,000. The apparent explanation is that in its eagerness to net experienced paralegals, law firms are willing to offer bonus salaries.

There is some justification in the many complaints about salary, however. One of the respondents to the East Bay survey wrote: "It bothers me, the great discrepancy between my salary and what the firm charges the client for my services. The work I do is professional—the client is billed a professional fee for my services—and yet I am paid a clerical salary. We are not idiots . . . we know what is going on . . . this bothers me both monetarily and ethically."

When you consider the rate at which paralegal services are billed to clients, this respondent has a point. One of the reasons law firms hire paralegals is that they can save clients money by billing them at a lesser hourly rate for paralegal service than for a lawyer's time. Generally the rate is about half. But when you consider that the going rate for lawyers in the larger metropolitan areas such as Los Angeles or New York City is now $100 to $125 per hour—and up to $225 in the more prestigious firms—it is apparent that paralegals bring in a lot of client money. The billing rate for paralegals in Los Angeles and New York City averages about $60 an hour, which translates into an income for the firm of $1800 a week if a paralegal devotes as much as thirty hours a week to billable client affairs. (Obviously paralegals do some work not directly related to client affairs, and therefore not billable to clients.) The sum of $1800 a week is $93,600 yearly income earned for the firm. A paralegal who earns only fifteen percent of that seems justified in feeling some resentment.

Actually the average paralegal probably does more than thirty hours a week of billable work, because overtime work is common. Most experienced paralegals I talked to estimated that they averaged sixty to seventy hours a week. Few received any compensation for overtime, particularly if their salary was $15,000 or more. Those who did receive compensation were not paid at overtime rates, but merely received their regular hourly rate.

The most thorough and comprehensive survey of paralegals I encountered while researching this book was the 1978 survey by the San Francisco Association of Legal Assistants. Prior to distributing its questionnaire in April 1978, the association canvassed all San Francisco law firms (excluding sole practitioners) and all corporations and banks with in-house legal departments. Questionnaires were then delivered to all paralegals known to be working in San Francisco, approximately 575. Responses were received from 225, or nearly 40 percent. Responses from voting members of the organization came to 67 percent.

The survey disclosed that San Francisco paralegals are surprisingly well educated. Sixty-five percent held bachelor's degrees and over 18 percent held master's degrees. Sixty-six percent had some type of formal paralegal training, and 40 percent of those had completed a legal assistance program.

Most respondents said they specialized in one area of the law. The most common specializations were civil litigation, corporate law, and estates and probate, with the first being reported four times as often as either of the other two. The second and third were reported by about an equal number of respondents. (The ABA survey conducted the same year showed much the same results nationally, except that real-estate specialists equalled the number of specialists in corporate law and in estates and probate.)

The amount of responsibility delegated to paralegals, the variety of tasks performed, working conditions, treatment by attorneys, and salary levels varied considerably. So did the degrees of satisfaction with their work expressed by respondents. Individual comments varied from near rapture over their jobs to total dissatisfaction. Here are some of the positive comments:

> I like working on my own, the freedom to make my own work schedule. I like writing letters, client contact, getting away from the office occasionally, and the diversity of my work.

Having worked in both a law firm and now within the legal department of a corporation, I feel extremely fortunate in my current position. The level of responsibility achieved in my current job is far above that ever permitted by the law firm. Although the pressure level is high at times, and the after hours committed to seeing a transaction through are many, the rewards have also been great.

I find the job stimulating; I like the responsibility and freedom.

I like my job because of the variety of tasks I can do. I don't feel as if I'm doing the same thing over and over again.

I am pleased with my profession, salary, and treatment by attorneys, secretaries, other legal assistants, and the legal community in general.

I very much enjoy my work as a legal assistant and plan to continue in the profession indefinitely.

Responsibility is enormous. Working conditions are pretty good. The work load varies, but usually I have plenty to do.

I would like more money, due to the fact that I do the majority of the work involved. Otherwise, I'm very pleased with the opportunities the corporation has provided me. Generally, good working conditions and wonderful attorneys who are very good at delegating responsibility and very understanding.

I like the independence and responsibility of my job. I am often assigned to do research, prepare legal memoranda, and draft documents.

There's lots of freedom, responsibility, and creativity allowed in my job, and my opinion is asked and valued.

I am very pleased with the development of my job into what I want: responsibility and independence from close supervision (since at this point I know as much if not more about probate than anyone else in the firm); a fairly good but not great salary; a pleasant working atmosphere. I am respected for my area of expertise by the attorneys in the firm and appreciate their coming to me for advice. I generally have complete responsibility for probating estates from beginning to end and have direct contact with clients and other professionals involved in the probate.

My job is usually varied and challenging. My firm sets no limits on the amount or the kinds of responsibility which may be delegated to legal assistants.

My job is challenging, varied, never routine, and I find that new assignments provide constant opportunities to learn and grow. I like and respect my attorney-supervisor and my co-workers. Working conditions are excellent; our office environment is comfortable, pleasant, and well-equipped.

It is an interesting job, performed under very pleasant working conditions, with knowledgeable and congenial personnel at all levels.

I like just about everything about my job. The attorneys with this firm are unusually fine people. I am treated by them as an equal.

There were some sour comments, too:

This job is a total waste of my time and the firm's money. Although considering what I am paid—the firm is not wasting that much.

My employers do not know how to utilize my skills; I

am often left with nothing to do. Many tasks I perform could be considered secretarial.

I've been quite disappointed in my job as a legal assistant. Despite the pleasant atmosphere of the firm and the friendliness of its employees, I have been given very little responsibility. After two years on the job, I expected more.

I feel that paralegaling is very boring and that there is no future in it, other than as an underling.

I think it is a misnomer to call a legal assistant a professional. The job, at least as I see it after more than four years of experience in financial district law firms, is a glorified clerical position.

Being a paralegal is very, very boring, and not advantageous financially.

I am leaving this position because I was hired as a paralegal, but do 95 percent secretarial work.

Although it is apparent from the comments received that about two thirds of the respondents were enthusiastic about their jobs, it is equally apparent that one third were not. One cannot tell whether or not similar results would be found in a national survey, because no such survey has yet been conducted. However, since local surveys on other aspects of paralegalism cited in this book tend to agree with the findings of the ABA's national survey, it seems probable that at least some degree of dissatisfaction with their jobs would be found among paralegals nationwide.

As one who many years ago resigned from an unrewarding job to venture into the highly speculative field of free-lance writing, it is difficult for me to understand why anyone dissatisfied with his job would continue in it. There are, of course, misfits in any profession, and probably some of the complainers would continue to complain even if moved from their present firms into one of those in which paralegals seem to be happy. But the tenor of most of the complaints indicates that the respondents *would* be happy under different working conditions.

My reaction to dissatisfied paralegals is to suggest looking for new jobs. As indicated earlier in this chapter, while brand-new paralegals may have trouble finding immediate employment in the larger metropolitan areas, there is a continuing and growing market for experienced paralegals. And it is not even necessary to give up the security of a present job in order to apply for a new one. Since two thirds of the firms covered by the San Francisco survey seem to be happy places to work, I can't help wondering why those employed by the other third make no attempt to change jobs.

The fringe benefits available in the paralegal profession are generally equivalent to those of employees in other professions. All of the paralegals I talked to personally (except those self-employed as free-lance paralegals) had health-insurance coverage and paid vacations. Some were covered by dental plans, and most received periodic bonuses. Vacations were generally two weeks after one year of employment, three weeks after two or three years.

The San Francisco survey showed that nearly 90 percent of the respondents were covered by medical plans, and over one third had dental plans. Seventy-four percent had employer-paid life-insurance policies. Paid vacations ran about the same as for those paralegals I interviewed personally. Forty-eight percent received bonuses, and an additional 26 percent, new employees, did not know whether or not they would receive them. Twenty percent were included by their employer in profit-sharing plans.

The material covered so far in this chapter has been a mixture of favorable and not-so-favorable aspects concerning the paralegal profession, with the favorable side winning. There is one negative point, though, that I must mention here.

If you are considering paralegal work as a step toward eventually becoming a lawyer (many paralegals enter the profession with that motive) you had better reconsider. In general, paralegal college credits are *not* transferable to law schools.

Many paralegals enter the profession in order to find out if a legal career is what they want before investing all the time and money required to go to law school. If you already have an associate or bachelor's degree and have to invest only in an extension course in paralegal studies, your experiment won't cost too much. In any event it will be considerably cheaper than going to law school, studying for and passing the bar examination, then discovering that the legal profession is not for you. A paralegal course such as the one at UCLA (where a bachelor's degree or equivalent legal experience is an entrance requirement) takes only twelve weeks full time or a year of evening school, and costs only a little over $1300.

However, if you plan to take a two- or four-year course in paralegal studies, you will be investing more time and money than it is worth if your motive is simply to find out if you would like to become a lawyer. If you plan on a permanent career as a paralegal, that is another matter, because in general the more formal training you have, the higher the salary you can expect. But if you do decide to go on to law school, you will still have three years of study ahead of you, regardless of whether you hold a certificate of completion from a twelve-week course or a four-year degree. Your college credits, or at least some of them, may be transferable to pre-law school, which usually is a two-year course, but none of them will be acceptable in law school itself.

Nevertheless, the paralegal profession *is* a profession, and society tends to give a certain amount of prestige to professional people. Right now you may encounter a lot of people who will be puzzled by the term "paralegal," and who will have to have it explained to them. But the field is expanding so rapidly that newspaper and magazine articles about it are educating the public more and more every day. Before long no one should have to question what you do when you say you are a paralegal. You can be proud of your career and proud of your work.

5

Paralegal Training

There are somewhere between 2500 and 3000 universities, colleges, junior colleges, and business schools teaching college-level courses in the United States. Since it was not feasible to send questionnaires to all of them, I compiled a list of 283 schools believed to give instruction in legal assistance, using information from state departments of education, the American Bar Association, and paralegal associations across the country.

Some of the schools had either been erroneously listed, or failed to reply to my query, but the remaining 257 schools, which are listed by states in Chapter 6, do offer paralegal training. I am sure this is not a complete list. Still, it is probably the most complete and accurate list published to date.

It probably won't be for long. The National Federation

of Paralegal Associations recently mailed out question-naires to 2200 colleges and universities in an attempt to obtain information on all paralegal training programs and publish a national directory.

Entrance requirements for the 257 schools responding to my survey varied all the way from none to a bachelor's degree. Most required either a high school diploma or a graduate equivalency diploma. Two required at least some college; fifteen required at least two years of college; twenty required a bachelor's degree; and nineteen required some work experience in a legal environment.

One hundred and thirty-two courses merely offered certificates; 116 offered associate degrees; and 29 offered bachelor's degrees. This adds up to more schools than responded, because in many cases schools offered a choice of courses leading to different diplomas. One school offered a master's degree in legal assistance.

The shortest course offered was a nine-week summer course at Newport College—Salve Regina, Newport, Rhode Island. There were 57 courses of less than six months, 28 of six to nine months, 40 one-year courses, 132 two-year courses, and 27 four-year courses. The one offering a master's degree required five and a half years of study.

Tuitions ranged all the way from nothing to over $5000 a year, but you shouldn't let that discourage you. So long as a student is willing to go somewhat in debt, college is available to virtually anyone with a decent high school average these days. Financial aid is so easily obtain-able in so many forms that most colleges and universities routinely include application forms for financial aid and lists of the various forms of aid available when they mail out school catalogs and registration application forms.

The United States Department of Education supports five programs of student assistance. For any of them a student must be a citizen or permanent resident of the United States, and must be enrolled or accepted for enrollment on at least a half-time basis. Renewal applications are required each year for all federal programs. The five federal programs are:

1. *The Basic Educational Opportunity Grants Program* (BEOG), which provides grants of from $200 to $1600 each academic year. These grants need not be repaid. Students are notified directly by the government within six weeks of application as to whether they are eligible. The notification is submitted to the college or university, which will then calculate the amount the student is eligible to receive. The amount of the award is based on the cost of attendance at the college.

2. *The Supplemental Educational Opportunity Grants Program* (SEOG). This program provides assistance to students with exceptional financial need, who, without the grant, would be unable to continue their education. Grants range from $200 to $1500 a year and must be matched with additional financial assistance from some other source (such as state aid or a scholarship, for example) at least equal to the amount of the grant. This grant also need not be repaid.

3. *The National Direct Student Loan Program* (NDSL), available to students who need loans to meet their educational expenses. A student may borrow up to a total of $2500 for a two-year program of study. Repayment normally begins nine months after the student graduates or leaves school for other reasons, at a minimum monthly payment of $30. No interest is charged until the repayment period begins, and then the interest amounts to only three percent of the unpaid balance. No repayments

are required for up to three years if the student serves in the armed forces, Peace Corps, or VISTA after leaving school.

This is the program that has received so much adverse publicity because of student defaults on loans. The federal government has recently launched a new get-tough policy to collect such unpaid loans, and has announced it will take full legal action to collect, including the garnisheeing of wages or, as a last resort, the turning over of accounts to professional collection agencies.

4. *The Guaranteed Student Loan Program* (GSL), which enables students to borrow directly from a bank, credit union, savings and loan association, or other participating lender in order to finance educational expenses. The maximum amount that may be borrowed is $2500 per academic year, at an interest rate of seven percent. The federal government will pay the interest on the loan until the beginning of the repayment period if the family's adjusted income is less than $25,000. Repayments normally begin between nine and twelve months after the student graduates or leaves school for other reasons, at a minimum monthly payment of $30. Deferments are available for certain situations. Detailed information and application forms are available directly from local banks and other lending institutions that participate in the program.

5. *The College Work-Study Program* (CWS). This program provides jobs for students who have great financial need and who must earn part of their educational expenses. In general, the salary received is the current minimum wage.

In addition, each state has student-assistance programs restricted to residents of the state. As random examples:

the State of Maryland sponsors fifteen different scholarship programs; the Pennsylvania Higher Education Assistance Agency administers both a scholarship and a loan program; New York State has a guaranteed loan program permitting students to borrow up to $2500 a year, as well as the New York State Tuition Assistance Program, which grants scholarships of from $100 to $1500 annually; California, despite charging no tuition to state residents at its chain of state universities and colleges, also offers several financial-aid programs to students.

It would take too much space to list each state's student-aid programs. This information is available in nearly all school catalogs, however, along with instructions on how to apply for financial aid.

On top of federal and state aid, private scholarships are available at virtually every college and university in the country. Again it would take too much space to attempt even a partial list of the types of scholarships available or the size of the monetary grants, but just to give you an example of how prevalent they are, the City College of San Francisco alone offers more than sixty different scholarships. If you are scholastically eligible for a scholarship at the college or university of your choice, it may amount to only some such small amount as $100 per year, or it may cover full tuition and other expenses.

The Standing Committee on Legal Assistants of the American Bar Association grants formal provisional approval and final approval to legal assistance courses that meet its standards. A course must be in operation for at least two years and must have graduated one class before approval is granted. The school is required to submit a self-evaluation report to the Standing Committee when it believes all the necessary conditions for approval have been met; then a team of representatives of the Standing Committee—usually three members—visits the college to make an inspection. If the inspection team is satisfied, approval is granted.

At the present time forty-five schools have ABA final approval, ten have provisional approval, and thirty-four more have applied for approval.

There is some controversy in the academic world as to whether or not seeking approval of the ABA for paralegal courses is appropriate. Many directors of such programs wrote me that they had no intention of applying for such approval, but that they had been approved by other bodies, which they deemed more proper agencies to grant approval. These sometimes were state or local bar associations, more often academic associations or state licensing agencies. This excerpt from a letter from the Coordinator of the Paralegal Studies Certificate Program of a major West Coast university was typical:

> Our school has consistently declined to seek approval from the ABA on the grounds that it is not the proper body to approve educational programs in this field; our program has the approval of the regular accrediting body in this region (Western Association of Schools and Colleges).

One school has even gone so far as to make a public attack on the ABA for daring to set itself up as the approving agency for paralegal courses. In June of 1978 the Paralegal Institute of New York City mailed the following letter countrywide to other schools offering paralegal training:

73

PARALEGAL INSTITUTE
132 Nassau Street
New York, N.Y. 10038
TO: Director, Career Planning And Placement
DATED: June 21, 1978
SUBJECT: Paralegal School Accreditation

You should know, to assist your students in the planning of their careers, that in New York State the only licensing authority for paralegal schools is the New York State Department of Education.

The American Bar Association, a trade association of lawyers, is not a licensing authority anywhere in the United States, and its recent program of giving ABA "approval" to paralegal schools has no authorization, and ABA "approval" has no meaning in the legal or academic communities. Neither the United States Office of Education (Tel: 202–245–2810) nor the Council of Postsecondary Education (COPA) (Tel: 202–245–1433) recognizes the ABA as an accrediting agency for paralegal schools, for reasons including the ABA's failure to have public representation; its conflict of interest with the paralegal field; the ABA's failure to include other interested groups (such as paralegals and paralegal associations) in its accrediting body; and the ABA body's lack of autonomy. For these reasons, the paralegal schools have no present accrediting agency, either federal or private, and the ABA's "approval" program is not only unauthorized, it appears to us and many others to be an illegal restraint of the paralegal field by the several lawyers running the program and the few institutions using the ABA's name to induce students to attend their schools.

If you have any questions, please give me a call, at 212–964–4705.

Carl E. Person, Director and
Member of the New York Bar

The Paralegal Institute offers a thirteen-week day course or a twenty-six-week evening course, which is not long enough to receive ABA approval. This is not necessarily a factor in Mr. Person's objection, however, since many educators share his view that the ABA is not the appropriate agency to approve paralegal courses. His reference to the "few institutions using the ABA's name to induce students to attend their schools" is hardly accurate, though. It may have been at the time the letter was written, but now eighty-nine schools, more than one third of all those in my survey, have either ABA final approval, provisional approval, or have applied for approval.

Although Mr. Person may have many schools on his side, paralegal associations in general, including the National Federation of Paralegal Associations, seem to regard the ABA as the appropriate body for approving paralegal courses. Since the ABA does not even suggest that its "approval" is anything more than just that, and does not in any way usurp the power of state licensing agencies and academic associations to "accredit" schools, the whole controversy tends to degenerate into a tempest in a teapot. ABA approval has no effect on a school's right to teach a course, but merely indicates that the course has met certain standards established by an interested agency with no official power.

The fact that so many schools apply for ABA approval seems to indicate it has at least some merit in their eyes. At worst, ABA approval does no harm that I can see.

The ABA and paralegal associations that have compiled lists of schools offering paralegal programs invariably append the disclaimer that they are not recommending any of the schools listed, but are merely offering the compilation as information. I have no such qualms. I am sure that the great majority of the schools listed in Chapter 6, and possibly all of them, offer adequate training. Many that lack ABA approval do have the approval of state or local bar associations, and in some cases the programs were instigated at the suggestion of and with the active cooperation of one or the other.

You will discover whether there is state or local bar sponsorship when you write for a catalog, because schools never fail to feature such sponsorship in their catalogs or brochures. If there is no mention of ABA approval, state or local bar association approval, or accreditation by some official agency, it is suggested that you contact either your local bar association or the nearest paralegal association for an evaluation of the school.

With the great choice of paralegal courses offered—sometimes even within the same school—the question arises as to just which one to take. That depends both on the time you have available and how far you expect to go in the paralegal profession. By far the greatest number of courses offered are two-year courses, most of which lead to an associate degree. But in the majority of cases the courses offered are tailored to the local needs of the legal profession, so that completion of any course should make you eligible for employment in that community.

It should be kept in mind that potential employers are usually familiar with the courses taught in local schools, and therefore will be quite aware of the type and amount of training you have when you apply for a job. The salary you will be offered and the type of work you will be given will naturally be colored by that knowledge. With a certificate showing that you have completed a six-month course in paralegal training, and with no other educational background except a high school diploma, you obviously are more likely to end up doing clerical work than legal work. With a two-year associate degree, you are much more likely to be hired as a bona fide paralegal. With a bachelor's degree, you would expect nothing less than a responsible position, even if your actual paralegal training amounted to only a short extension course on top of your BA or BS. With a bachelor's degree in paralegal training, you will be in the most elite group of job seekers, and can justifiably insist on a job compatible with your training at a decent starting salary.

Paralegal training is not universally available throughout the country. As nearly as I could determine, seven states have no schools offering courses: Arkansas, Idaho, Maine, Montana, North Dakota, South Dakota, and Wyoming. Ten have only one school each offering paralegal studies: Alaska, Hawaii, Nebraska, Nevada, New Hampshire, Rhode Island, Utah, Vermont, West Virginia, and Wisconsin. Six have only two schools: Georgia, Kentucky, Louisiana, New Mexico, South Carolina, and Tennessee.

California has the most schools, with thirty-two. Texas is second with seventeen, New York third with fifteen, Michigan fourth with twelve. Florida has eleven, Missouri and Pennsylvania have ten each. (Actually, Pennsylvania has thirty-three, but twenty-four are branches of the same school: Pennsylvania State University.) Colorado, Massachusetts, New Jersey, North Carolina, and Virginia each have seven schools offering paralegal training. Connecticut, Illinois, and Washington each have six. Arizona, Kansas, Maryland, and Ohio each have five. Alabama, the District of Columbia, Indiana, Iowa, and Minnesota each have four. Delaware, Mississippi, Oklahoma, and Oregon each have three.

Receiving a catalog and an application-for-admission

form in the mail from any of the schools listed in Chapter 6 does not automatically ensure your admission, even if you meet the basic entrance requirements. Many courses admit only a certain number of students. Therefore, you would be wise to get your application in as early as possible in order to avoid the disappointment of learning that the class was already full when it arrived.

You may also discover that entrance requirements are somewhat stiffer than they appear to be from the data given in the next chapter. Because of the necessity for briefness, only the most basic data could be listed. When a high school diploma is listed as a requirement for admission, for example, that is indicated by the abbreviation HS without any elaboration. But as often as not, it is required that you must have graduated at a certain level of your class.

For instance, both Winona State University of Minnesota and the Central Pennsylvania Business School show that a high school diploma is needed for admission. But Winona, which grants a bachelor's degree after a four-year course, requires entrants to be in the upper half of their class. Central Pennsylvania Business School, which offers an associate degree, prefers them to be in the upper fourth.

All schools look for applicants with intelligence, industry, and ability to learn. Paralegalism is not a profession for mediocre talent. Even at schools where there are no strict entrance requirements, certain necessary qualities in the individual are stressed. Typical is this statement about the admission policy from the "Paralegal Careers" brochure of Kirkwood Community College, Cedar Rapids, Iowa:

Kirkwood considers the total individual in granting admission to college programs. There are no required admission tests, and past academic performance is not an admission consideration. Kirkwood does require that you have completed high school, or a G.E.D. program, or that you are a "mature adult" when you apply.

But then under the heading PERSONAL QUALI-TIES, the brochure appends this:

The following are individual characteristics that are considered desirable for students preparing to be legal assistants:
—An ability to question and to think critically.
—An interest in the processing of documents.
—A high level of language skills and comprehension.
—A thorough and conscientious concern for detail.
—An ability to draft documents with minimal guidance
—An ability to establish rapport with people.

School after school lists similar requirements in different terms. The constant stress is that schools are looking for superior talent for their paralegal programs.

That is hardly surprising, since it is a demanding, highly technical profession.

Some of the tuitions listed in the next chapter are for the 1979–1980 school year. Others are for the 1978–1979 school year. But since costs are steadily rising, it is advisable to expect a ten- to twenty-percent increase per year over the tuitions quoted.

6

The Schools

Four categories of information are given after each school listed:

a. Entrance requirements. For the sake of brevity, only basic information is given. Thus the abbreviation HS (high school diploma) doesn't necessarily mean that all high school graduates are acceptable. In many cases an applicant must be in the upper one half, upper one third, or even in the upper one fourth of the class. Similarly ACT (American College Test) or SAT (Scholastic Aptitude Test) doesn't merely mean that you must pass such tests, but usually means that you must make a certain score well above average. Even where "None" is listed, an applicant will be rejected if his answers on the application-for-admission form, or the impression he makes on his counselor, peg him as an obvious misfit.

b. Duration of course. This is given in weeks, months, or years for courses involving full-time study. But in extension or evening courses, where the work is spread out over a period of time on a part-time basis, the duration is usually given in CH (credit hours). As a rule of thumb, thirty to thirty-six credit hours are equivalent to a year of full-time study. Many schools have abandoned summer vacations and operate on a full-time basis the year round. At these schools terms are often called "quarters." Actually, in most cases, there are only three "quarters" to a school year, so they are really thirds, or trimesters. At such schools two years of work are compressed into a year and a half, which is why an associate degree may be earned in a year and a half at some schools on the list, whereas it takes two years at others. In Washington State, though, there really are four terms in a school year, and credit hours are thus based on a quarter, rather than a trimester. In that state, therefore, you will find 90 CH listed as necessary for an associate degree instead of the usual 60 to 72, and 180 CH required for a bachelor's degree instead of the usual 120 to 144.

c. Tuition. Unless otherwise indicated, basic tuition only is listed. Additional fees and books may run another $200 a year. At schools away from your home, where you will have to live in a dormitory, room and board are an additional expense. All tuitions shown are for one year, or for the duration of the course if it is less than one year.

d. Certificate or degree offered. C, AD, or BD (respectively standing for certificate, associate degree, or bachelor's degree) are the three most common awards granted at the end of courses. Different schools give their certificates different titles, such as Legal Assistance Certificate, Certificate of Paralegal Studies, or a variety of other

81

names. All have been lumped under the symbol "C" simply to cut down on the number of abbreviations required. For the same reason, associate of arts degrees, associate of science degrees, and associate of arts and science degrees (generally granted after a two-year course) are all listed simply as AD, for associate degree. Similarly bachelor of arts degrees and bachelor of science degrees are both lumped under the designatiion BD, for bachelor's degree.

In many cases, schools offer more than one type of course, leading to more than one type of diploma. In such cases, the data for the shortest course is always listed first. For example, the first school on the list, Alabama University at Montgomery, has this information following it: (a) HS or EE; (b) 2 or 4 yr; (c) $700; (d) C or BD.

Translated, this means that (a) entrance requirements are a high school diploma or an entrance examination; (b) two courses are offered, one running two years, the other four; (c) tuition is $700 a year; (d) the two-year course brings a certificate, the four-year course a bachelor's degree.

The following symbols and abbreviations are used:

*	ABA final approval
**	ABA provisional approval
***	ABA approval has been applied for
ACT	American College Test
AD	Associate degree
BD	Bachelor's degree
C	Certificate
CC	Certificate of completion
CH	Credit hours

col	College
corres	Correspondence school
D	Daytime course
EE	Entrance examination
equiv	Equivalent
Ev	Evening course
exp	Experience
GED	Graduate equivalency diploma
HS	High school diploma
incl	Includes
leg	Legal
leg empls	Legal employees
leg exp	Legal experience
leg sec	Legal secretary
mo	Month
NDA	No data available
NR	Nonresident
paras	Paralegals
PI	Personal interview
RC	Resident of city or county
RS	Resident of state
SAT	Scholastic Aptitude Test
Sats	Saturdays

SCHOOLS BY STATES

ALABAMA

Auburn University at Montgomery, School of Sciences, Dept. of Criminal Justice, Montgomery, AL 36117 (a) HS or EE; (b) 2 or 4 yr; (c) $700; (d) C or BD.

**Samford University, Paralegal Studies, 800 Lakeshore Dr.,

83

Birmingham, AL 35209 (a) HS or EE; (b) 2 yr Ev or 4 yr; (c) Ev $37.50 CH—D $60 CH; (d) AD or BD.

Spring Hill College, Mobile, AL 36608 (a) HS or EE; (b) 2 or 4 yr; (c) $2600; (d) C or BD.

University of South Alabama, School of Continuing Education, Office of the Dean, Mobile, AL 36608 (a) HS; (b) 2 yr; (c) $500 to $750; (d) C.

ALASKA

Anchorage Community College, 2533 Providence Ave., Anchorage, AK 99504 (a) HS; (b) 2 yr; (c) $20 CH; (d) AD.

ARIZONA

*Northern Arizona University, Legal Assistant Program, Box 15044, Flagstaff, AZ 86001 (a) PI; (b) 4 yr; (c) NDA; (d) BD.

***Paralegal Schools, Inc., 3201 North 16th St., Suite 11, Phoenix, AZ 85016 (a) Some col or exp; (b) 6 mo; (c) $1550; (d) C.

***Phoenix College, 1202 W. Thomas Rd., Phoenix, AZ 85013 (a) HS or GED; (b) 2 yr; (c) RC $90—RS $950—NR $1450; (d) AD.

Scottsdale Community College, 9000 E. Chaparral Rd., P.O. Box Y, Scottsdale, AZ 85252 (a) HS or GED + ACT; (b) 2 yr; (c) RC $90—RS $950—NR $1430; (d) AD.

***The Sterling School, 1010 E. Indian School Rd., Phoenix, AZ 85014 (a) 45 CH & PI; (b) 6 mo; (c) $1350; (d) C.

CALIFORNIA

American College of Paramedical Arts & Sciences, 1800 N. Broadway, Santa Ana, CA 92706 (a) HS & EE; (b) 1 yr; (c) $2350; (d) C.

American Legal Services Institute, 2719 Canada Blvd., Glendale, CA 91208 (a) 1 yr col; (b) 9 to 15 mo corresp.; (c) $950; (d) C.

***American River College, 4700 College Oak Dr., Sacramento, CA 95841 (a) None; (b) 2 yr; (c) None; (d) C.

California State College, San Bernardino, Coordinator Paralegal Studies, Dept. of Political Science, 5500 State College Parkway, San Bernardino, CA 92407 (a) HS or 18; (b) 1 yr; (c) None; (d) C.

California College of Paralegal Studies, 6832 Van Nuys Blvd., Van Nuys, CA 91405 (a) HS or 2 yr leg exp; (b) 12 wks or 1 yr; (c) $1580; (d) C.

California State University—Chico, Chico, CA 95929 (a) HS or 18; (b) 23 CH; (c) None; (d) C.

*California State University at Los Angeles, 5151 State University Dr., Los Angeles, CA 90032 (a) HS; (b) 1 yr Ev; (c) none; (d) C.

Canada College, 4200 Farm Hill Blvd., Redwood City, CA 94061 (a) 1 yr col or 6 mo leg exp; (b) 2 yr; (c) None; (d) C.

***Cerritos College, 11110 E. Alondra Blvd., Norwalk, CA 90650 (a) HS or 18; (b) 1 or 2 yr; (c) None; (d) C or AD.

*City College of San Francisco, 50 Phelan Ave., San Francisco, CA 94112 (a) HS; (b) 1 or 2 yr; (c) None; (d) C or AD.

***Coastline Community College, 10231 Slater Ave., Fountain Valley, CA 92708 (a) HS or 18; (b) 1 or 2 yr; (c) None; (d) C or AD.

Criss College of Business, c/o Glendale University, 220 N. Glendale Ave., Glendale, CA 91206 (a) NDA; (b) 11 wk Ev; (c) NDA; (d) C.

Dominican College of San Rafael, San Rafael, CA 94901 (a) BD; (b) 1 yr; (c) $2580; (d) C.

Fresno City College, 1101 E. University Ave., Fresno, CA 93741 (a) HS or 18; (b) 2 yr; (c) None; (d) AD.

Humphreys College, 6650 Inglewood Dr., Stockton, CA 95207 (a) HS; (b) 2 yr; (c) $1600; (d) AD.

Imperial Valley College, P.O. Box 158, Imperial, CA 92251 (a) HS or 18; (b) 1 or 2 yr; (c) None; (d) C or AD.

Los Angeles City College, 855 N. Vermont Ave., Los Angeles, CA 90029 (a) HS or 18; (b) 2 yr; (c) None; (d) AD.

*Merritt College, 12500 Campus Dr., Oakland, CA 94619 (a) HS; (b) 6 mo or 2 yr; (c) None; (d) C or AD.

Pacific Legal Arts College, 1387 Del Norte Rd., Camarillo, CA 93010 (a) EE; (b) 2 yr Ev; (c) NDA; (d) C.

Pasadena City College, Business Dept., 1570 E. Colorado Blvd., Pasadena, CA 91106 (a) HS or 18; (b) 2 yr D or Ev; (c) RC None—NR $1540; (d) C or AD.

**St. Mary's College, Legal Assistant Program A, P.O. Box 52, Moraga, CA 94575 (a) 2 yr col; (b) 4 quarters D or Ev; (c) $3132; (d) C.

San Francisco State University, Continuing Education, 1600 Holloway Ave., San Francisco, CA 94132 (a) 56 CH or equiv leg exp; (b) 15 wks Ev; (c) $1110; (d) C.

*UCLA, University Extension, Attorney Assistant Training Program, Dept. of Human Development & Services, Room 214, 10995 LeConte Ave., Los Angeles, CA 90024 (a) BD or equiv leg exp; (b) 18 wks D—1 yr Ev; (c) $1310 incl. books & fees; (d) C.

University of California at Berkeley, University Extension, 2223 Fulton St., Berkeley, CA 94720 (a) Working leg secs or paras; (b) 3 mo Sats & Ev; (c) $200; (d) CC.

***University of California at Irvine, Certificate Program in Legal Asistance, Irvine, CA 92717 (a) BD or 2 yr leg exp; (b) 2 yr; (c) $850; (d) C.

University of La Verne, 1950 3rd St., La Verne, CA 91750 (a) Leg Sec or PI; (b) 2 yr; (c) $55 CH; (d) C.

**University of San Diego, Lawyer's Assistant Program, Alcala Park, San Diego, CA 92110 (a) BD; (b) 12 wk; (c) $1225; (d) C.

***University of Santa Clara, Institute for Paralegal Education, Center for Continuing Education, Santa Clara, CA 95053 (a) BD; (b) 1 yr; (c) $2400; (d) C.

*University of Southern California, The Law Center and the College of Continuing Education, Administration Bldg., Room 354, Los Angeles, CA 90007 (a) HS; (b) 18 CH; (c) $2520; (d) C.

*University of West Los Angeles, School of Paralegal Studies, 10811 West Washington Blvd., Culver City, CA 90230 (a) 15 CH or equiv leg exp—or 2 yr col; (b) 21 wks or 2 yr; (c) $1195 or $2490; (d) C or BD.

Valley College of Paralegal Studies, 10911 Riverside Dr., N. Hollywood, CA 91602 (a) Leg exp or HS + PI; (b) 11 wk or 1 yr; (c) $350 or $1400; (d) C.

West Valley College, 14000 Fruitvale Ave., Saratoga, CA 95070 (a) HS or 18; (b) 2 yr; (c) None; (d) AD.

COLORADO

*Arapahoe Community College, 5900 S. Sante Fe Dr., Littleton, CO 80120 (a) BD or equiv leg exp—or HS + EE; (b) 1 or 2 yr; (c) RS $342—NR $1263; (d) C or AD.

Community College of Denver, Auraria Campus, 11 W. Colfax, Denver, CO 80204 (a) HS or 18; (b) 1 or 2 yr; (c) RS $337—NR $1484; (d) C or AD.

Colorado Paralegal Institute, 609 W. Littleton Blvd., Suite 201, Littleton, CO 80120 (a) BD or 4 yr leg exp; (b) 8 mo; (c) $120; (d) C.

Denver Paralegal Institute, 908 Central Bank Bldg., 1108 15th St., Denver, CO 80202 (a) BD or 3 yr leg exp; (b) 4 mo D or 9 mo Ev; (c) $1620; (d) C.

El Paso Community College, 2200 Bolt Ave., Colorado Springs, CO 80904 (a) 2 yr leg exp; (b) 1½ yr; (c) NDA (d) C.

Pikes Peak Community College, 5675 S. Academy Blvd., Colorado Springs, CO 80906 (a) HS + leg exp; (b) 1½ yr; (c) RS $225—NR $896; (d) C.

University of Denver College of Law, Program of Advanced Professional Development, 200 W. 14th Ave., Denver, CO 80204 (Restricted program; refresher & update courses for paralegals already working. No other data available.)

CONNECTICUT

**Manchester Community College, 60 Bidwell St., Manchester, CT 06040 (a) None; (b) 2 yr; (c) RS $354; (d) AD.

Mattatuck Community College, Legal Assistant Program, 750 Chase Parkway, Waterbury, CT 06708 (a) None; (b) 2 yr; (c) RS $250—NR $950; (d) AD.

***Norwalk Community College, 333 Wilson Ave., Rte 136, Norwalk, CT 06854 (a) HS; (b) 2 yr; (c) SR $250—NR $950; (d) AD.

Post Junior College, 800 County Club Rd., Waterbury, CT 06708 (a) HS + ACT + PI; (b) 2 yr; (c) $3772; (d) AD.

***Quinnipiac College, Legal Studies Program, Hamden, CT 06518 (a) HS + SAT; (b) 4 yr; (c) $3400; (d) BD.

*Sacred Heart University, P.O. Box 6460, Bridgeport, CT 06606 (a) HS + EE; (b) 2 yr; (c) NDA; (d) AD.

DELAWARE

Goldey Beacom College, 4701 Limestone Rd., (Rte 7), P.O. Box 5047, Wilmington, DE 19808 (a) HS; (b) 2 yr; (c) $920; (d) AD.

University of Delaware, Legal Assistant Education Program, 2800 Pennsylvania Ave., Wilmington, DE 19806 (a) HS; (b) 6 courses; (c) $702; (d) C.

***Wesley College, Dover, DE 19901 (a) HS + SAT or ACT; (b) 1 or 2 yr, D or Ev; (c) $3050; (d) C or AD.

DISTRICT OF COLUMBIA

*Antioc School of Law, Legal Technician Program, 1624 Crescent Pl., NW, Washington, DC 20009 (a) 20; (b) 6 mo—1 yr—1½ yr; (c) $1600 ea 6 mo; (d) C.

*Georgetown University, School for Summer & Continuing Education, Washington, D.C. 20057 (a) BD or equiv leg exp, (b) 3 10-wk sessions Ev; (c) $1250; (d) C.

*George Washington University, Legal Assistant Program, College of General Studies, 2130 H St. NW, Suite 621, Washington, DC 20052 (a) BD or equiv leg exp; (b) 15 wk Sats—or 1 yr Ev; (c) $1500; (d) C.

Southeastern University, 501 Eye St. SW, Washington, DC 20024 (a) HS + EE; (b) 2 yr; (c) $1800; (d) AD.

FLORIDA

Broward Community College, 3501 Southwest Davie Rd., Fort Lauderdale, FL 33314 (a) HS; (b) 2 yr; (c) NDA; (d) AD.

Florida Atlantic University, Institute for Legal Assistants, Center for Management & Professional Development, Boca Raton, FL 33431 (a) 2 yr col; (b) 11 mo Ev; (c) $1200 incl all fees; (d) C.

Florida Junior College at Jacksonville, Downtown Campus, 101 W. State St., Jacksonville, FL 32202 (a) HS; (b) 2 yr; (c) $378; (d) AD.

**Florida Technological University, Allied Legal Services Program, Dept. of Political Science, P.O. Box 25000, Orlando, FL 32816 (a) HS; (b) 1 or 4 yr; (c) $720; (d) C or BD.

Hillsborough Community College, P.O. Box 22127, Tampa, FL 33622 (a) HS; (b) 2 yr; (c) RS None—NR $465; (d) AD.

***Langley Paralegal Institute, 315 Hyde Park Ave., Tampa, FL 33606 (a) 2 yr col or equiv leg exp; (b) 4 mo; (c) $1500; (d) C.

Manatee Junior College, Dept. of Criminal Justice, Urban Studies & Health Occupations, Bradenton, FL 33506 (a) HS; (b) 2 yr; (c) SR $468—NR $936; (d) AD.

Miami-Dade Community College, Downtown Campus, 300 NE 2nd Ave., Miami, FL 33132 (a) HS; (b) 2 yr; (c) SR $420—NR $870; (d) AD.

*Sante Fe Community College, P.O. Box 1530, 3000 NW 83rd St., Gainesville, FL 32602 (a) EE; (b) 63 CH Ev; (c) NDA; (d) AD.

Southern Career Institute, 1580 NW 2nd Ave., Drawer 2158, Boca Raton, FL 33432 (a) HS; (b) 3 mo to 2 yr corresp; (c) $495; (d) C.

University of West Florida, Alpha College, Pensacola, FL 32504 (a) BD; (b) 1½ yr; (c) $16.50 CH; (d) BD in Legal Assistance.

GEORGIA

*National Center for Paralegal Training, Lawyer's Assistant Program, 3376 Peachtree Rd. NE, Suite 430, Atlanta, GA 30326 (a) BD; (b) 12 wk D—25 wk Ev; (c) $1225; (d) CC.

Paralegal Institute, Columbia Southern School of Law, 1904

90

Monroe Dr., Atlanta, GA 30324 (a) BD or 5 yr leg exp; (b) 6 mo Ev; (c) $1186; (d) C.

HAWAII

*Kapiolani Community College, 620 Pensacola St., Honolulu, HI 96814 (a) HS + EE; (b) 2 yr; (c) $90 incl fees (d) AD.

ILLINOIS

MacCormac Junior College, 327 S. LaSalle St., Chicago, IL 60604 (a) HS or EE; (b) 2 yr; (c) $2175; (d) AD.

*Mallinckrodt College, 1041 Ridge Rd., Wilmette, IL 60091 (a) 1½ yr col or HS + EE; (b) 18 CH Ev—2 or 4 yrs D; (c) $200 per course; (d) C—AD or BD.

Midstate College, Jefferson at Liberty, Peoria, IL 61602 (a) HS; (b) 1 yr; (c) $840; (d) C.

*Roosevelt University, Lawyers Assistant Program, 430 S. Michigan Ave., Chicago, IL 60605 (a) BD; (b) 12 wk D or Ev; (c) $1250; (d) C.

***Sangamon State University, Center for Legal Studies, Springfield, IL 62708 (a) PI; (b) 4 or 5½ yr; (c) NDA (d) BD or MA.

*William Rainey Harper College, Algonquin & Roselle Rds., Palatine, IL 60067 (a) HS + EE; (b) 18 CH or 2 yr; (c) $15 CH; (d) C or AD.

INDIANA

Ball State University, Dept. of Political Science, Muncie, IN 47306 (a) NDA; (b) 2 or 4 yr; (c) $280; (d) AD or BD.

***Indiana Central University, 1400 East Hanna Ave., Indianapolis, IN 46227 (a) HS + SAT or ACT; (b) 2 yr; (c) $2640 incl all fees; (d) AD.

*University of Evansville, P.O. Box 329, Evansville, IN 47702
(a) HS + PI + SAT; (b) 2 or 4 yr; (c) $1750 (d) AD or BD.

Vincennes University, 1002 N. First St., Vincennes, IN 47591
(a) HS or EE; (b) 2 yr; (c) RC $620—NR $650 to $1550; (d) AD.

IOWA

Des Moines Area Community College, 2006 S. Ankeny Blvd.,
Ankeny, IA 50021 (a) HS + EE; (b) 2 yr; (c) $450; (d) AD.

**Iowa Lakes Community College, 300 S. 18th St., Estherville,
IA 51334 (a) HS; (b) 2 yr; (c) $500; (d) AD.

Kirkwood Community College, Dept. of Business, 6301 Kirkwood Blvd. SW, P.O. Box 2068, Cedar Rapids, IA 52406 (a)
HS or GED; (b) 2 yr; (c) RS $480—NR $720; (d) AD.

Marycrest College, 1607 W. 12th St., Davenport, IA 52804 (a)
HS + ACT or SAT; (b) 47 CH or 65 CH; (d) $2850; (d) C or
AD.

KANSAS

**Barton County Community College, Great Bend, KS 67530
(a) HS + ACT or SAT; (b) 2 yr; (c) $320; (d) AD.

Hutchinson Community Junior College, 1300 N. Plum St.,
Hutchinson, KS 67501 NDA

***Johnson County Community College, Paralegal Program,
College Blvd. at Quivers Rd., Overland Park, KS 66210 (a) HS
or GED; (b) 1 or 2 yr; (c) RS $450—NR $1050; (d) C or AD.

Washburn University, 1700 College Ave., Topeka, KS 66621
(a) HS; (b) 2 yr; (c) $650; (d) AD.

Wichita State University, College of Business Administration,
Wichita, KS 67208 (a) 24 CH; (b) 2 yr; (c) RS $510—NR $1500;
(d) C.

KENTUCKY

***Eastern Kentucky University, Legal Assistant Program, Richmond, KY 40475 (a) HS; (b) 2 or 4 yr; (c) $500; (d) AD or BD.

Midway College, Midway, KY 40347 (a) HS + ACT + EE + PI; (b) 1 or 2 yr; (c) $1500; (d) C or AD.

LOUISIANA

Louisiana State University at Shreveport, LA 71101 (a) HS; (b) NDA; (c) NDA; (d) NDA.

Tulane University, University College, New Orleans, LA 70118 (a) EE + PI; (b) 1 yr Ev; (c) $1600; (d) C.

MARYLAND

Community College of Baltimore, Liberty Campus, 2901 Liberty Heights Ave., Baltimore, MD 21215 (a) HS + ACT + PI; (b) 12 CH or 2 yr; (c) RC $360—NR $720 to $1080; (d) C or AD.

Dundalk Community College, 7200 Sollers Point Rd., Baltimore, MD 21222 (a) HS; (b) 2 yr; (c) RS $9 CH—NR $18 to $38 CH; (d) AD.

Paralegal Institute, 914 Silver Spring Ave., Silver Spring, MD 20910 (a) 2 yr col; (b) 4 mo D—11 mo Ev; (c) $1485; (d) C.

University of Maryland, University College, Paralegal Studies, Conferences and Institutes Division, College Park, MD 20742 Gives only a noncredit short course. No other data available.

*Villa Julie College, Legal Assistant Program, Greenspring Valley Rd., Stevenson, MD 21153 (a) HS + PI; (b) 2 yr; (c) $1850; (d) AD.

MASSACHUSETTS

Anna Maria College, Paxton, MA 01612 (a) HS; (b) 2 yr; (c) $1450; (d) C.

***Bay Path Junior College, Longmeadow, MA 01106 (a) HS; (b) 2 yr; (c) $3050 incl noon meal; (d) AD.

*Bentley College, Institute of Paralegal Studies, Beaver & Forest Sts., Waltham, MA 02154 (a) 2 yr col or equiv leg exp; (b) 13 wk; (c) $1175; (d) C.

Boston State College, 625 Huntington Ave., Boston, MA 02115 NDA

Middlesex Community College, Division of Continuing Education, P.O. Box T, Bedford, MA 01730 (a) None; (b) 15 CH Ev; (c) $375; (d) C.

University of Massachusetts at Boston, Boston, MA 02116 (a) HS + SAT or ACT; (b) 2 or 4 yr; (c) RS $1050—NR $3100; (d) C or BD.

Regis College, Box 27, Weston, MA 02193 (a) BD or Junior status toward BD; (b) 1 to 1½ yr Ev to complete 6 courses; (c) $225 per course; (d) C.

MICHIGAN

Baker Junior College of Business, 1110 Eldon Baker Dr., Flint, MI 48507 (a) HS or EE; (b) 1½ yr; (c) $1500; (d) AD.

*Ferris State College, Big Rapids, MI 49307 (a) HS; (b) 2 yr; (c) RS $696—NR $1680; (d) AD.

Grand Valley State Colleges, School of Public Service, Allendale, MI 49401 (a) HS + ACT; (b) 4 yr; (c) SR $810—NR $1845; (d) BD.

Henry Ford Community College, 5101 Evergreen Rd., Dearborn, MI 48128 (a) None; (b) 62 CH Ev; (c) RC $12 CH—NR $21 CH; (d) AD.

Hillsdale College, Hillsdale, MI 49242 (a) HS + SAT or ACT; (b) 4 yr; (c) $3390; (d) BD + C.

Kellogg Community College, 450 North Ave., Battle Creek, MI 49016 (a) HS or 18; (b) 2 yr; (c) RC $15 CH-NR $25 to $38 CH; (d) AD.

Lansing Community College, Accounting and Office Programs Dept., 419 N. Capitol Ave., P.O. Box 40010, Lansing, MI 48901 (a) None; (b) 2 yr; (c) RC $495—RS $625.50—NR $1215; (d) AD.

Macomb County Community College, South Campus, 14500 Twelve Mile Rd., Warren, MI 48093 (a) 18; (b) 41 or 62 CH; (c) NDA; (d) C or AD.

***Madonna College, 36600 Schoolcraft Rd., Livonia, MI 48150 (a) HS; (b) 2 or 4 yr; (c) $42 CH; (d) AD or BD.

***Charles Stewart Mott Community College, Business Division, 1401 E. Court St., Flint, MI 48503 (a) HS; (b) 2 yr; (c) $558; (d) AD.

*Oakland University, Division of Continuing Education, Rochester, MI 48063 (a) NDA; (b) Choice of 6 10-wk courses or a 14-wk course, all Ev; (c) $420; (d) C.

Southwestern Michigan College, Cherry Grove Rd., Dowagiac, MI 49047 (a) HS; (b) 2 yr; (c) RC $420—RS $540—NR $690; (d) AD.

MINNESOTA

*Inver Hills Community College, 8445 College Trail, Inver Grove Heights, MN 55075 (a) HS + ACT or SAT; (b) 1½ yr; (c) $660; (d) AD.

***North Hennepin Community College, 7411 85th Ave. North, Minneapolis, MN 55445 (a) Must complete basic law course + PI; (b) 2 yr; (c) $540; (d) AD.

*University of Minnesota, Twin Cities General College, 216

Pillsbury Dr. SE, Minneapolis, MN 55455 (a) HS + PI; (b) 90 CH D or Ev; (c) NDA; (d) C, but may be combined with AD or BD.

*Winona State University, Winona, MN 55987 (a) HS + ACT; (b) 4 yr; (c) RS $510—NR $1015; (d) BD.

MISSISSIPPI

***Northwest Mississippi Junior College, Senatobia, MS 38668 (a) HS; (b) 2 yr; (c) RC $370—RS $460—NR $970; (d) AD.

University of Southern Mississippi, Paralegal Studies, P.O. Box 5108, Southern Station, Hattiesburg, MS 39401 (a) NDA; (b) 4 yr; (c) NDA; (d) BD.

University of Mississippi, Dept. of Extension, MI 38677 NDA

MISSOURI

***Avila College, 11901 Wornall Rd., Kansas City, MO 64145 (a) HS + SAT or ACT; (b) 4 yr; (c) $1950; (d) BD.

Columbia College, Legal Assistant Program, Columbia, MO 65201 (a) 2 yr col; (b) 2 yr; (c) $2500; (d) BD + C.

Maryville College, 13550 Conway Rd., St. Louis, MO 63141 (a) HS + SAT or ACT; (b) 4 yr; (c) $2650; (d) BD.

Missouri Western State College, 4525 Downs Dr., St. Joseph, MO 64507 (a) HS; (b) 1 or 2 yr; (c) NDA; (d) C or AD.

Penn Valley Community College, 3201 Southwest Trafficway, Kansas City, MO 64111 (a) None; (b) 1 or 2 yr; (c) $230; (d) C or AD.

*Rockhurst College, Evening Division, 5225 Troost Ave., Kansas City, MO 64110 (a) HS; (b) 18 CH Ev; (c) $720; (d) C.

St. Louis Community College at Florissant Valley, 3400 Pershall Rd., St. Louis, MO 63135 (a) HS or 18; (b) 1 or 2 yr; (c) RC $17 CH—RS $42 CH—NR $54 CH; (d) C or AD.

St. Louis Community College at Meramec, 11333 Big Bend Blvd., Kirkwood, MO 63122 (a) HS or 18; (b) 36 or 65 CH Ev; (c) RC $18 CH—NR $36 CH; (d) C or AD.

***Stephens College, Columbia, MO 65201 (a) HS; (b) 4 yrs; (c) $5200 incl board & room; (d) BD.

*William Woods College, Fulton, MO 65251 (a) HS + ACT or SAT; (b) 4 yr; (c) $3475; (d) BD.

NEBRASKA

*Lincoln School of Commerce, 1821 K St., P.O. Box 82826, Lincoln, NE 68501 (a) HS + EE; (b) 1½ yr; (c) $400 total; (d) AD.

NEVADA

Reno Business College, Wells & Wonder, Reno, NV 89502 (a) HS; (b) 36 or 96 CH; (c) $700; (d) C or BD.

NEW HAMPSHIRE

Rivier College, Nashau, N.H. 03060 (a) HS; (b) 2 or 4 yr; (c) $2200; (d) AD or BD.

NEW JERSEY

*Burlington County College, Pemberton-Browns Mills Rd., Pemberton, NJ 08068 (a) HS; (b) 64 CH Ev; (c) RC $17 CH— RS $19 CH—NR $68 CH; (d) AD.

*Cumberland County College, Social & Behavorial Science Dept., P.O. Box 517, Vineland, NJ 08360 (a) HS + NJ Basic Skills Test; (b) 2 yr; (c) RC $500—RS $1000—NR $1700 (d) AD.

First School of Secretarial & Paralegal Studies, 516 Main St., East Orange, NJ 07078 (a) HS or GED; (b) 4 mo D—8 mo Ev; (c) $1352; (d) C.

***Mercer County Community College, 1220 Old Trenton Rd., P.O. Box B, Trenton, NJ 08690 (a) HS; (b) 2 yr; (c) $576; (d) AD.

Ocean County College, College Dr., Toms River, NJ 08753 (a) HS; (b) 1 or 2 yr; (c) RC $500—RS $1000—NR $2000; (d) C or AD.

Plaza School, Garden State Plaza, Rte 17 & Rte 4, Paramus, NJ 07552 (a) BD; (b) 12 wk; (c) NDA; (d) C.

***Upsala College, Paralegal Program, Office of Continuing Education, East Orange, NJ 07019 (a) BD; (b) 8 mo; (c) $975; (d) C.

NEW MEXICO

American Indian Law Center, The University of New Mexico School of Law, 1117 Stanford NE, Albuquerque, NM 87131 (a) Must be American Indian with a reservation address + HS or GED; (b) 7 mo; (c) None; (d) Diploma.

University of Albuquerque, St. Joseph's Pl. NW, Albuquerque, NM 87140 (a) PI; (b) 2 yr; (c) $2050; (d) AD.

NEW YORK

*Adelphi University, The Lawyer's Assistant Program, Center for Career Programs, Garden City, L.I., NY 11530 (a) BD + PI; (b) 12 wk D—6 mo Ev; (c) $1325; (d) C.

Broome Community College, Paralegal Assistant Program, P.O. Box 1017, Binghamton, NY 13902 (a) For working leg empls only; (b) 30 or 60 CH Ev; (c) $27 CH; (d) C or AD.

Elizabeth Seton College, 1061 N. Broadway, Yonkers, NY 10701 (a) HS + PI; (b) 2 yr; (c) $2200; (d) AD.

Herkimer County Community College, Herkimer, NY 13350 (a) HS + SAT or ACT; (b) 2 yr; (c) RS $550—NR $1100; (d) AD.

*Hilbert College, 5200 S. Park Ave., Hamburg, NY 14075 (a) HS + PI; (b) 2 yr; (c) $1700; (d) AD.

Junior College of Albany, 140 New Scotland Ave., Albany, NY 12208 (a) EE + PI; (b) 2 yr; (c) $2100; (d) AD.

***Long Island University (Two locations)
Paralegal Studies Program, Room M500
Long Island University/Brooklyn Center
University Plaza
Brooklyn, NY 11201

Paralegal Studies Program
The White Plains Center/Mercy College
Martine Ave. & S. Broadway
White Plains, NY 10601
(a) BD + PI; (b) 12 wk D—24 wk Ev; (c) $1215 incl fees; (d) C.

Marist College, Poughkeepsie, NY 12601 (a) 1 yr col or equiv leg exp; (b) 36 CH Ev; (c) $3456; (d) C.

Nassau Community College, Paralegal Assistant Program, Stewart Ave., Garden City, NY 11530 (a) HS; (b) 2 yr; (c) CR $730; (d) AD.

New York University, School of Continuing Education, Institute of Paralegal Studies, 332 Shimkin Hall, Washington Square, New York, NY 10003 (a) AD; (b) 1 yr; (c) $1512; (d) Diploma in Paralegal Education.

Paralegal Institute, 132 Nassau St., New York, NY 10038 (a) PI; (b) 13 wk D—26 wk Ev; (c) $1395 incl all expenses; (d) CC.

Schenectady County Community College, Washington Ave., Schenectady, NY 12305 (a) HS; (b) 2 yr; (c) NDA; (d) AD.

Suffolk County Community College, Selden Campus, 533 College Rd., Selden, NY 11784 (a) HS; (b) 2 yr D or Ev; (c) RS $660—NR $1320; (d) AD.

Syracuse University, University College, 610 E. Fayette St., Syracuse, NY 13202 (Planning program in near future.)

NORTH CAROLINA

Central Carolina Technical Institute, Dept. of Community Colleges, 1105 Kelly Dr., Sanford, NC 27330 (a) HS; (b) 2 yr; (c) RS $210—NR $625 incl all expenses; (d) AD.

Central Piedmont Community College, P.O. Box 4009, Charlotte, NC 28204 (a) None; (b) 1½ yr; (c) RS $3.25 CH—NR $16.50 CH; (d) AD.

Davidson County Community College, P.O. Box 1287, Lexington, NC 27292 (a) HS; (b) 2 yr; (c) $186; (d) AD.

*Fayetteville Technical Institute, P.O. Box 5236, Fayetteville, NC 28303 (a) HS; (b) 2 yr.; (c) RS $117—NR $595; (d) AD.

Greensboro College, Greensboro, NC 27420 (a) HS + SAT; (b) 2 or 4 yr; (c) $2070; (d) C or BD.

Pitt Technical Institute, Police Science & Paralegal Dept., P.O. Drawer 7007, Greenville, NC 27834 (a) HS or GED; (b) 2 yr; (c) $140; (d) AD.

Southwestern Technical Institute, P.O. Box 95, Sylva, NC 28779 (a) HS; (b) 2 yr; (c) RS $136—NR $693: (d) AD.

OHIO

Capital University Law School, Center for Special & Continuing Legal Education, Columbus, OH 43209 (a) BD or 2 yr col + 1 yr leg exp + PI; (b) 9½ mo Ev; (c) $975; (d) C.

Dyke College, 1375 E. 6th, Cleveland, OH 44114 (a) BD or HS + ACT; (b) 6 CH or 4 yr; (c) NDA; (d) C or BD.

***Ohio Paralegal Institute, 1001 Euclid Ave., Cleveland, OH 44115 (a) HS or GED + EE; (b) 9 mo; (c) $2320 incl all fees; (d) C.

Sinclair Community College, 444 W. 3rd St., Dayton, OH 45402 (a) HS + EE; (b) 2 yr; (c) RC $11 CH—RS $16 CH—NR $21 CH; (d) AD.

University of Toledo, University Community & Technical College, Counseling, Guidance & Advising Center, Scott Park Campus, 2801 W. Bancroft St., Toledo, OH 43606 (a) HS + EE; (b) 2 yr; (c) $1090; (d) AD.

OKLAHOMA

*Oscar Rose Junior College, 6420 SE 15th St., Midwest City, OK 73110 (a) HS + ACT; (b) 2 yr; (c) RS $250—NR $760; (d) AD.

***Tulsa Junior College, 909 S. Boston Ave., Tulsa, OK 74119 (a) HS + ACT + PI; (b) 2 yr; (c) $293; (d) AD.

*University of Oklahoma, Continuing Legal Education Law Center, 300 Timberdell Rd., Room 314, Norman, OK 73019 (a) HS; (b) 2 or 4 yr; (c) $600 1st yr—$980 2nd yr; (d) C or BD.

OREGON

Lane Community College, 4000 E. 30th Ave., Eugene, OR 97405 (a) None; (b) 2 yr; (c) $264; (d) AD.

*Mount Hood Community College, 26000 SE Stark St., Gresham, OR 97030 (a) HS or 18; (b) 2 yr; (c) RC $390—RS $630—NR $1500; (d) AD.

*Portland Community College, 12000 SW 49th Ave., Portland, OR 97219 (a) PI—prefer leg employees; (b) 45 or 72 CH; (c) NDA; (d) C or AD.

PENNSYLVANIA

Cedar Crest College, Legal Assistant Program, Allentown, PA 18104 (a) HS; (b) 4 yr; (c) $3500; (d) BD + C.

Central Pennsylvania Business School, College Hill, Summerdale, PA 17093 (a) HS; (b) 1⅔ yr; (c) $2475; (d) AD.

Gannon College, Perry Square, Erie, PA 16501 (a) HS + ACT or SAT; (b) 2 yr; (c) $2250; (d) AD.

Harrisburg Area Community College, 3300 Cameron Street Rd., Harrisburg, PA 17101 (a) HS or GED; (b) 1 or 2 yr; (c) RC $500; (d) C or AD.

*The Institute for Paralegal Training, 235 S. 17th St., Philadelphia, PA 19103 (a) BD + EE; (b) 3 mo; (c) $1295; (d) CC.

King's College, Wilkes-Barre, PA 18711 (a) HS or GED; (b) 60 CH D or Ev; (c) $68 CH or $2600 full time; (d) AD.

***Main Line Paralegal Institute, 121 N. Wayne Ave., Wayne, PA 19087 (a) PI; (b) 4 mo summer session or 10 mo Ev; (c) $1185; (d) C.

Northhampton County Area Community College, 3835 Green Pond Rd., Bethlehem, PA 18017 (a) None; (b) 24 CH Ev; (c) NDA; (d) C.

Pennsylvania State University, College of Buisness Administration, 310 Business Administration Building, University Park, PA 16802 (a) None; (b) 10–15 wks; (c) $450; (d) C. (Twenty-four campuses.)

Ogontz Campus, 1600 Woodland Rd., Abbington, PA 19001

Allentown Campus, 725 Ridge Ave., Allentown, PA 18102

Altoona Campus, Smith Bldg., Altoona, PA 16603

DuBois Campus, College Place, DuBois, PA 15801

Behrend College, Station Rd., Erie, PA 16501

Hazleton Campus, Highacres, Hazleton, PA 18201

Penn State University, Continuing Education, C101 Milton S. Hershey Medical Center, Hershey, PA 17033

Penn State University, Continuing Education, 649 S. Henderson Rd., King of Prussia, PA 19406

McKeesport Campus, University Dr., McKeesport, PA 15132

Delaware County Campus, 25 Yearsley Mill Rd., Media, PA 19063

Capitol Campus, Rte. 230, Middletown, PA 17057

Beaver Campus, Brodhead Rd., Monaca, PA 15061

Mont Alto Campus, Mont Alto, PA 17237

New Kensington Campus, 3550 Seventh Street Rd., New Kensington, PA 15068

Berks Campus, R.D. 5, Tulpehocken Rd., Reading, PA 19608

Schuylkill Campus, State Highway, Schuylkill Haven, PA 17972

Worthington Scranton Campus, 120 Ridge View Dr., Dunmore, PA 18512

Shenango Valley Campus, 147 Shenango Ave., Sharon, PA 16146

Penn State University, Continuing Education, 341 Dartmouth Ave., Swarthmore, PA 19081

Fayette Campus, P.O. Box 519, Rte. 119 North, Uniontown PA 15401

Penn State University, Continuing Education, 309 Shields Building, University Park, PA 16802

Wilkes-Barre Campus, P.O. Box 1830, Wilkes-Barre, PA 18708

Penn State University, Continuing Education, 208 Terminal Bldg., Montoursville, PA 17754

York Campus, 1031 Edgecomb Ave., York, PA 17404

*Widener College, Chester, PA 19013 (a) 2 yr col or leg exp; (b) 3 mo summer session or 8 mo Ev; (c) $1175; (d) C.

RHODE ISLAND

The Newport College, Salve Regina, Newport, RI 02840 (a) HS + PI; (b) 9 wk; (c) $1200; (d) C.

SOUTH CAROLINA

Greenville Technical College, P.O. Box 5616 Station B, Greenville, SC 29606 (a) EE + PI; (b) 2 yr; (c) RS $225—NR $450; (d) AD.

***Midlands Technical College, P.O. Drawer Q, Columbia, SC 29250 (a) None; (b) 2 yr; (c) RC $330—RS $411—NR $660; (d) AD.

TENNESSEE

*Cleveland State Community College, Legal Services, Cleveland, TN 37311 (a) HS; (b) 2 yr; (c) RS 252—NR $1198; (d) AD.

University of Tennessee, College of Business Administration, Knoxville, TN 37916 (Program in process of formation.)

TEXAS

Dallas County Community College District, 701 Elm St., Dal-

las,TX 75202 (a) HS or 18; (b) 2 yr; (c) RC $120—RS $440—NR $1200; (d) AD.
(Seven campuses.)

Brookhaven College, 3839 Valley View Lane, Farmers Branch, TX 75234

Cedar Valley College, 3030 North Dallas Ave., Lancaster, TX 75134

Eastfield College, 3737 Motley Dr., Mesquite, TX 75150

El Centro College, Main & Lamar Sts., Dallas, TX 75202

Mountain View College, 4849 W. Illinois Ave., Dallas, TX 75211

North Lake College, 2000 Walnut Hill Lane, Irving, TX 75062

Richland College, 12800 Abrams Rd., Dallas, TX 75234

*Del Mar College, Legal Assistant Dept., Baldwin & Ayers, Corpus Christi, TX 78404 (a) HS + ACT; (b) 2 yr; (c) RS $190; (d) AD.

El Paso Community College, 6601 Dyer St., El Paso, TX 79904 (a) Nonc; (b) 2 yr; (c) $100; (d) AD.

***Houston Community College System, Legal Assistant Program, 4310 Dunlavy Ave., Suite 225, Houston, TX 77006 (a) HS or GED; (b) 68 CH Ev; (c) $11 CH; (d) AD.

Lamar University, Division of Public Services, P.O. Box 10008, Beaumont, TX 77710 (a) HS; (b) 2 yr; (c) $280; (d) C.

San Antonio College, 1300 San Pedro Ave., San Antonio, TX 78284 (a) HS + SAT or ACT; (b) 2 yr; (c) $128 to $400; (d) AD.

Southwest Texas State University, Lawyers Assistant Program, San Marcos, TX 78666 (a) BD + PI; (b) 1 semester; (c) $200; (d) C.

***Southwestern Paralegal Institute, 5512 Chaucer Dr., Houston, TX 77005 (a) BD or equiv leg exp; (b) 12 wk D—32 wk Ev; (c) $1350; (d) C.

***Texas Paralegal School, Inc., 819 Main St., Suite 203, Dallas, TX 75202 (a) EE; (b) 9 mo; (c) $2000; (d) C.

**Texas Paralegal School, 608 Fannin, Suite 1903, Houston, TX 77002 (a) EE + PI; (b) 9 mo; (c) $2500; (d) C.

West Texas State University, School of Business, Dept. of Business Education & Office Administration, Canyon, TX 79016 (a) 2 yr col or leg exp; (b) 2 yr; (c) RS $120—NR $1200; (d) C.

UTAH

**Utah Technical College at Provo, Legal Assistant Program. P.O. Box 1009, Provo, UT 84601 (a) None; (b) 2 yr; (c) RS $292—NR $722; (d) C or AD.

VERMONT

Woodbury Associates, School of Continuing & Legal Education, P.O. Box 736, 3 West St., Montpelier, VT 05602 (a) NDA; (b) 1 yr; (c) NDA; (d) C.

VIRGINIA

Ferrum College, Ferrum, VA 24088 (Offers major in Business Administration with a minor in Paralegal.) (a) HS; (b) 2 yr; (c) $3490 incl room & board; (d) AD.

J. Sargeant Reynolds Community College, Parham Campus, P.O. Box 12084, Richmond, VA 23173 (a) HS + PI; (b) 47 CH Ev; (c) RS $400—NR $1316; (d) C.

Paralegal Institute, 6801 Whittier Ave., McLean, VA 22101 (a) 2 yr col; (b) 4 mo D—11 mo Ev; (c) $1485; (d) C.

Tidewater Community College (a) HS or GED; (b) 1 yr; (c) RS $400—NR $1340; (d) C. (Three locations.)

Tidewater Community College, Chesapeake Campus, 1428 Cedar Rd., Chesapeake, VA 23320

Tidewater Community College, Frederick Campus, State Rte. 135, Portsmouth, VA 23703

Tidewater Community College, Virginia Beach Campus, 1700 College Crescent, Virginia Beach, VA 23456

**University of Richmond, University College Evening School, Richmond, VA 23173 (a) 2 yr col or recommended by attorney; (b) 36 CH Ev; (c) $1728; (d) C.

WASHINGTON

Central Washington State College, Ellensburg, WA 98926 (a) HS + ACT; (b) 4 yr; (c) $591; (d) BD.

City College, Administrative Offices Bldg., Seattle, WA 98104 (a) None; (b) 90 or 180 CH; (c) $130; (d) AD or BD.

*Edmonds Community College, 20000 68th Ave. West, Lynnwood, WA 98036 (a) HS or 18; (b) 90 CH; (c) RS $306—NR $1188; (d) AD.

Fort Steilacoom Community College, 9401 Farwest Dr. SW, Tacoma, WA 98498 (a) Employee of leg office; (b) 2 yr; (c) $202; (d) AD.

*Highline Community College, South 240th & Pacific Highway South, Midway, WA 98031 (a) HS or 18; (b) 2 yr; (c) RS $306—NR $1188; (d) AD.

Spokane Community College, Evening Division, North 1810 Greene St., Spokane, WA 99207 (a) PI; (b) 47 or 92 CH; (c) RS $66; (d) C or AD.

WEST VIRGINIA

Community College of Marshall University, Huntington, WV 25701 (a) SAT; (b) 2 yr D or Ev; (c) RS $550—NR $1300; (d) AD.

WISCONSIN

*Lakeshore Technical Institute, 1290 North Avenue, Cleveland, WI 53015 (a) HS; (b) 2 yr; (c) $279 1st yr—$324 2nd yr; (d) AD.

7

Jobs and Wages

In studying the data furnished in this chapter the reader should take into consideration the fact that the job situation in any particular area may be constantly changing. In addition, with an annual inflation rate of over 10 percent in the United States, you may have to add 10 to 20 percent to the salaries quoted. Nevertheless, any broad trend is probably reflected with some degree of accuracy.

Although employment opportunities are much poorer in some states than in others, and are almost nonexistent in a few, there seems to be a steadily growing job market that can probably absorb most graduates of paralegal training courses for at least the next few years. As might be expected, the heaviest job market and the largest salaries are found in the big metropolitan areas, where law firms are larger, and where there are many corporate legal departments. Jobs can be also be found (usually at lower salaries) in smaller communities, and even in some rural areas, as more and more attorneys learn the advantages of employing paralegals.

In general, however, the time when you could land a paralegal job without any formal training or experience is over. Today, with schools graduating an adequate supply of trained paralegals, law firms and legal departments of corporations don't have to bother with in-house training, and more and more are insisting that applicants be graduates of recognized training programs. (Actually, many law firms and legal departments continue to have in-house training programs in specialized fields for paralegals, legal secretaries, and even their junior lawyers, but that is another matter. Such courses are designed to improve the knowledge of already trained professionals, not to teach them the basics of their jobs.)

Many schools have their own job-placement services, which actively explore employment sources and refer graduates for jobs. For the most part they are highly effective, with from 80 to 100 percent of graduates being placed.

Other schools give instruction in job hunting as part of their programs. One of the best is at the National Center for Paralegal Training in Atlanta, Georgia, which conducts what it calls a Pre-Employment Orientation Program. This includes training in how to prepare a résumé, how to prepare for a personal interview, and how to make a good impression on a prospective employer.

EMPLOYMENT OPPORTUNITIES BY STATES

ALABAMA

The only data received came from the two schools in the Mobile area, which reported that salaries in that community for paralegals with four-year college degrees ranged from $10,200 to $13,200. No information on the availability of jobs could be obtained.

ALASKA

Some jobs available. No data on salaries.

ARIZONA

Phoenix: Two different sources reported job opportunities excellent in the Phoenix area. One cited a salary range of from $9000 to $12,000, the other gave a median salary of $9500.

Scottsdale: Few paralegal jobs are available in this relatively small community (population about 75,000). Those who have jobs earn from $12,000 to $13,000 if they hold two-year college degrees and from $13,000 to $15,000 if they hold four-year degrees.

No information from other parts of Arizona was received.

ARKANSAS

No information, but since there are neither any paralegal schools in Arkansas nor any paralegal associations, it may be assumed that the job market, if any, is poor.

CALIFORNIA

Data came in from twelve different localities in California. The statewide picture seems to be that employment prospects are fairly good. These are the individual areas that reported:

Fresno: Fresno City College reported that the area demand for paralegals was strong enough for the college to place 100 percent of its graduates. The median salary was estimated to be $12,000.

Imperial Valley: It was guessed that this community of about 80,000 could absorb only about five new paralegals a year for the next few years.

Los Angeles: Data came in from many sources here, much of it conflicting. The most accurate source was probably paralegal Debbie Korman, the employment coordinator for the Los Angeles Paralegal Association, since she gathers job information for the *Los Angeles Paralegal Association Reporter*, the association's monthly newsletter. In a sense she conducts an ongoing survey. Debbie feels that although employment opportunities for paralegals with experience are excellent in the Los Angeles area, opportunities for new paralegals are only fair. Salaries varied according to experience, with these ranges:

To start	$8500 to $10,000
1 year experience	$9500 to $11,000
2 years experience	$10,000 to $12,000
3 years experience	$14,000 to $15,000
4 years experience	$15,000 to $16,000
5 years experience	$15,000 to $19,000

She reported that on the west side of the city, in such

exclusive areas as Westwood and Century City, salaries were higher.

Moraga: St. Mary's College reported that 100 percent of its first class of paralegals, graduated in 1978, obtained positions, and that placements in the north California area have been high ever since. Salaries range from $9600 to $10,800.

Norwalk: No information on the availability of jobs was received, but starting salaries were reported to be $9600 and up; salaries for paralegals with experience range from $14,400 to $18,000.

Oakland: The East Bay Association of Legal Assistants conducted a comprehensive survey in 1978, which has been cited in chapter 4. One of the findings was that the availability of jobs for new paralegals are fairly limited, but that the field is growing steadily and the future looks brighter. According to Jane Lamont, President of the EBALA, many firms that hired one paralegal two years ago are now employing four or five.

Average starting salaries were $9000 to $10,200, about the same as in the Los Angeles area, but a few went as high as $16,000 to $16,800. For paralegals with from one to three years experience, salaries ranged from $10,800 to $15,600. With six years or over, they were $15,900 to $16,800. Nearly seven percent of all respondents reported salaries of from $16,800 to $17,100.

After the survey was tabulated, 25 percent of the respondents reported that they had received raises ranging from $600 to $1800 a year. That made the corrected average salary of all those surveyed approximately $13,300.

Orange County: The only report from this area was from the University of California—Irvine. Orange

County is an extremely conservative area, and seems to be somewhat behind the rest of California in its acceptance of paralegals. The field is just beginning to emerge in this area. The school had no hard data on job availability, but reported that law firms were beginning to contact the university to interview students for jobs on graduation. Starting salaries ranged from $10,800 to $12,000.

Pasadena: Jobs are readily available at from $9000 to $18,000.

San Francisco: The 1978 survey conducted by the San Francisco Association of Legal Assistants has been previously mentioned in the book. It was an unusually thorough survey, in which questionnaires were sent to all paralegals known to be working in San Francisco (approximately 575). Sixty-seven percent of the association's voting members responded and nearly 45 percent of the total surveyed replied. Salaries varied widely, ranging all the way from $3900 a year (for part-time work) to $28,800. The median starting salary for full-time work was $10,200, but the high starting salary—$24,000—was greater than the median salary even for paralegals with six years experience. Median salaries for experienced paralegals were:

1 year experience	$12,000
2 years experience	$13,050
3 years experience	$13,350
4 years experience	$13,500
5 years experience	$15,000
6 or more	$15,600

The survey did not address the question of job availability, but from other sources it appears that the situation is much the same as in Los Angeles and Oakland: the job market for beginners was a little tight, but good for experienced paralegals.

San Rafael: Dominican College reported few jobs in San Rafael (the community has only about 40,000 people) but a good market for its graduates in nearby larger communities, such as Santa Rosa, Oakland, and San Francisco. In Marin County there were a few independent paralegal contractors who were billing at from $7.50 to $10 an hour.

Saratoga: A single source reported that employment opportunities in Santa Clara Valley were quite good, but had no pay data.

Stockton: Humphreys College reported that there is a growing demand for paralegals in the area, and many of its students are placed before finishing college. The only pay data available was that a paralegal's pay exceeds that of a legal secretary by a significant amount.

COLORADO

Information was received concerning only two areas in Colorado.

Denver: Reports conflicted. The several schools in that area reported a good job market, with starting salaries ranging from $9500 to $15,000. The Rocky Mountain Legal Assistants Association, headquartered in Denver, says the job market is very tight and training and experience are essential. It reported starting salaries ranging from $8400 to $10,000, with yearly increases of anywhere up to $2500.

Littleton: A survey conducted by one of the schools showed job opportunities in both the public and private sectors. Starting salaries averaged $9600.

CONNECTICUT

Hamden: Job opportunities are increasing, but no salary data was available.

Norwalk: Most law offices in the area are small, but are beginning to show an interest in paralegals, and they may be a major source of jobs soon. A few large firms employ paralegals at salaries from $11,000 to $25,000. Many corporations have legal departments that employ paralegals, paying them from $11,000 to $13,000.

Waterbury: Job opportunities are poor but are improving. Jobs start as low as $7500. Nearby larger communities pay paralegals up to $17,000 to $18,000.

DELAWARE

Jobs with private law firms seem to be mostly in the northeastern part of the state. Specific information about only two localities was received:

Dover: Most paralegal jobs are in the public sector, with state and local agencies. The average starting salary is $8500.

Wilmington: The starting wage averages $8000, but experienced paralegals earn $15,000 to $16,000. No information on the availability of jobs was received.

DISTRICT OF COLUMBIA

Washington, D.C.: The job market is excellent here because federal agencies employ a lot of paralegals and the city has many large law firms. Georgetown University reported that 90 percent of its paralegal graduates in 1978 obtained jobs locally. Starting salaries ranged from $10,000 to $12,000.

FLORIDA

Gainesville: A 1978 survey by Santa Fe Community College showed a good job market with salaries up to $15,000.

Miami: No verifiable information was available.

Pensacola: The job market for new paralegals is a little tight, but a good potential market is predicted for the near future as more lawyers learn how to use paralegals advantageously. No salary figures were received.

Tampa: The job market here is steadily growing. A median starting salary of $9000 was reported.

GEORGIA

Atlanta: A 1978 survey by the Georgia Association of Legal Assistants, headquartered in Atlanta, made the interesting finding that 64 percent of the employers of paralegals in Atlanta planned to hire additional paralegals within the next year. A 1979 statewide survey of 322 paralegals found these average salaries (evened off to the nearest $50):

	Within Metro-Atlanta	*Outside Metro-Atlanta*
To start	$10,350	$ 9,050
1 year experience	$11,300	$ 9,250
2 years experience	$12,350	$10,000
3 years experience	$13,600	$11,600
4 years experience	$13,950	No Data
5 years experience	$17,050	No Data
6 years experience	$17,300	$12,100

HAWAII

Honolulu: Good job opportunities, with starting salaries ranging from $7200 to $9000. The top salary reported by an experienced paralegal was $13,200.

IDAHO

No information, but since there are neither any paralegal schools nor paralegal associations in Idaho, it may be assumed that the job market, if any, is poor.

ILLINOIS

Chicago: A 1978 survey by the Illinois Paralegal Association, headquartered in Chicago, showed a range of salaries from $9500 to $21,000, which included starting salaries as well as paralegals with twenty years experience. Average salaries were $13,000 to $15,000. This survey didn't address the question of job availability, but information from other sources indicates this is a good job market.

Springfield: Sangamon University reports that it has so far graduated only a few from its four-year paralegal course, but that all graduates have found jobs. The positions listed include law librarian, a job with the Community Action Committee in Lincoln, and one with the Office of the Speaker, Illinois House of Representatives. Because Springfield is the state capital, public-sector jobs are available, and there are also a number of large law firms. Salaries range from $12,000 to $14,000. Some students do part-time work before they graduate.

Wilmette: Salaries range from $10,000 to $20,000. No information on job availability was received.

118

INDIANA

Evansville: There are fair job opportunities here. Starting salaries range from $8000 to $10,000.

Indianapolis: There is not a strong job market here, but some jobs are available. Salaries range from $10,000 to $12,000.

Muncie: A good job market. Salaries to start average $9000; for those with experience they run to $15,000.

IOWA

Information was received from only two communities, and they did not include the state's major city, Des Moines.

Cedar Rapids: Kirkwood Community College reports no problem in placing graduates in the area. Starting salaries range from $9000 to $14,000.

Estherville: Iowa Lakes Community College reports that jobs are just beginning to open up, but there is already sufficient local demand so that graduates have no difficulty finding employment. Starting salaries average $10,000.

KANSAS

The following information is mainly from the Kansas Legal Assistants Society, headquartered in Tecumseh, with additional information from several schools.

Kansas City and Wichita are the only areas with metropolitan atmosphere and outlook. The remainder of the state, including Topeka, has a rather rural or small-town atmosphere. This makes for pleasant living conditions, but also for a conservatism slow to accept change. Smaller communities are just beginning to use paralegals, but interest is growing.

Great Bend: Paralegals are being used more and more. Benton County Community College surveyed two hundred law firms, banks, and other businesses with legal departments in the county. The response was positive. Many schools have asked the college to refer job applicants to them.

Hutchinson: A slowly growing job market. No salary information was received.

Kansas City (including both Kansas City, Kansas and Kansas City, Missouri): Job opportunities are limited, but increasing rapidly. There are more applicants than available jobs at present, but as in most metropolitan areas, the use of paralegals is steadily increasing. Paralegals with both training and experience have no difficulty finding jobs, but it is a tight market for inexperienced paralegals, even with training. Salaries range from $9000 to $18,000.

Topeka: A poor job market. As the seat of Washburn Law School, the city is crowded with young attorneys willing to work at a paralegal's wages, plus law students wanting part-time work in law offices. The KLAS estimates that there are no more than ten paralegals in the whole city, with salaries ranging from $7200 to $15,600, most in the range of $8400 to $10,800. Washburn University, however, classes job opportunities as excellent, with starting salaries at about $8000.

Wichita: The best job market in the state, but the trend is to hire only formally trained paralegals, with some legal experience preferred. There is a shortage of applicants with those qualifications. Salaries range from $10,800 to $15,600.

120

KENTUCKY

Midway College at Midway conducted a statewide survey in 1977. This showed fifty-five paralegals in about six hundred law firms, only eight with formal paralegal training. This information is so out-of-date, though, that it is practically meaningless, since two college classes have graduated since then. Both the number of paralegals and the number with formal training must have grown considerably since then.

The concentration of paralegals seems to be in the Lexington and Louisville areas. There were fair employment prospects in both cities, but no heavy demand. Salaries started about $9000, averaged about $12,000 with experience, and went as high as $18,000.

LOUISIANA

New Orleans: The job market here is excellent, but formal training is necessary. The average starting salary is $11,000.

No information was received from the rest of the state.

MAINE

No data available.

MARYLAND

The only information received was from Villa Julie College, at Stevenson, which reports starting wages in the Baltimore area run from $8500 to $12,000. No information on the availability of jobs was furnished.

MASSACHUSETTS

The Massachusetts Paralegal Association, headquartered in Boston, reports that the number of paralegals employed throughout the Commonwealth, except in the Boston area, is growing steadily in both the public and private sectors. Previous experience is valuable but not essential in getting jobs.

Boston: The Massachusetts Paralegal Association classifies the job market in Boston as "particularly tight." However, Bentley College of Waltham reported that 97 percent of the graduates of its most recent class found work in the Boston area within three months of graduation. Starting salaries range from $9100 to $14,500.

MICHIGAN

Big Rapids: A 1978 survey of the 1977 graduating class of Ferris State College showed that of thirty-three graduates, eighteen were employed in paralegal jobs, eight were continuing their education, and only three were looking for work. The other four did not respond to the survey. Starting salaries were $6750 to $9960.

Dowagiac: There are only a few local jobs available, and the pay is low, from $6700 up.

Flint: Salaries range from $7800 to $15,600. No information on the availability of jobs was received.

Livonia: Good opportunities at $10,000 to $17,000.

Rochester: A job seekers market. Starting wages range from $9500 to $14,000. With experience, some exceed $20,000.

MINNESOTA

Data from only two communities were received.

Inver Grove Heights: Inver Hills College has graduated only eleven paralegal students to date, but all are employed. The average starting salary is $9000.

Winona: Winona State University reported that all graduates wishing paralegal jobs have been placed. For the 1977 graduating class of seventeen, the school placement service had requests from fifty prospective employers. Starting salaries were $8500 to $10,000. The highest current salary reported was $13,000.

MISSISSIPPI

A survey conducted by the Northwest Mississippi Junior College of Senatobia, covering all of Mississippi plus Memphis, Tennessee, found that 75 percent of all law firms foresee hiring paralegals in the near future. Starting salaries statewide range from $7000 to $9000.

MISSOURI

Columbia: Columbia College reports it graduated only five from its paralegal course in 1978. Two went on to graduate school, the other three got jobs at an average starting salary of $12,500.

Kansas City: Avila College in Kansas City reports that many requests for paralegals are received by its placement service. The Kansas City Association of Legal Assistants says that Kansas City is still a good place to look for a job, and that new jobs are opening up all the time. Rockhurst College of Kansas City says that an average of one new opening a month is reported to it.

(See also comments about Kansas City under KAN-SAS.)

St. Louis: Not a heavy job market, but jobs are available on a limited basis. Starting salaries range from $10,000 to $14,000.

MONTANA

No information was received, but since Montana has no paralegal schools or paralegal associations, it may be assumed that the job market, if any, is extremely limited.

NEBRASKA

Lincoln: The job market is good, with starting salaries ranging from $6600 to $9600.

No information was received from other parts of the state.

NEVADA

No information available.

NEW HAMPSHIRE

No information available.

NEW JERSEY

East Orange: Jobs are available at $9100 to $11,700 according to one source, from $12,000 to $16,000 according to another.

Toms River: An Ocean County feasibility study in 1977 showed fifty-two paralegal jobs per year opening up in the county at an average starting salary of $7000 to $8000. Although this study is somewhat outdated, job opportunities in the area still seem to be good.

Trenton: Mercer County Community College has so far graduated only five paralegals. Four are working in law offices at starting salaries of $9000 to $10,000. The fifth is going to a four-year college.

No other usable information on New Jersey was received.

NEW MEXICO

Albuquerque: The area is just beginning to respond to the paralegal concept. Employment is moderately available. No data on wages were received.

Since there are no large metropolitan areas in New Mexico other than Albuquerque, employment prospects throughout the rest of the state are poor.

NEW YORK

Buffalo: The job market is highly competitive, with formal training necessary and experience recommended. Starting salaries range from $7500 to $10,000.

Herkimer: Herkimer County Community College reports that 100 percent of its 1977 class was employed in 1978. The average pay was $10,500.

New York City: There is a good job market here. Starting salaries range from $10,000 to $13,500.

Schenectady: Most law firms here are small. In the past they have been reluctant to use paralegals, but they are gradually opening up, so that there is a potential job market. Starting salaries are very low, though, ranging from $5200 to $6350.

Seldon: A good job market, with starting salaries around $9000.

White Plains: Job opportunities are very good, both in

White Plains and in nearby Manhattan. Starting salaries in White Plains are $10,000 to $10,600. For Manhattan salaries, see *New York City*.

Yonkers: Westchester County corporations are just starting to hire paralegals for their legal departments, which makes the area a brand-new job market. Starting salaries average $8000.

NORTH CAROLINA

Across the state paralegal jobs seem to be plentiful, with starting salaries ranging from $8000 to $14,000.

Fayetteville: Jobs were readily available locally for graduates of the Fayetteville Technical Institute up until last year, but now graduates have to go to larger cities for employment.

Greenville: Jobs are available at starting salaries of from $7800 to $9100.

Lexington: Jobs are available. Starting salaries range from $8500 to $11,000.

Sylva: Job openings are limited locally, but Southwestern Technical Institute reports its graduates have no difficulty finding jobs in larger communities.

NORTH DAKOTA

No information was received, but since the state has no paralegal schools and no paralegal associations, it can be assumed that the job market, if any, is poor.

OHIO

Cleveland: A good and growing job market, with starting salaries of from $8000 to $10,000.

No information was received about other parts of the state.

OKLAHOMA

Statewide many jobs are opening up in the legal departments of oil-producing companies.

Tulsa: Tulsa Junior College's course is so new that in 1979 no one has yet graduated, but potential employers have already begun to ask for referrals. Anticipated starting salaries are from $8200 to $10,600.

Midwest City: Paralegal jobs are readily available at starting salaries between $8400 and $12,000.

OREGON

Only 150 paralegals are employed in the whole state, and only one of those is formally "certified" under that state's certification program.

Eugene: Poor employment opportunities.

Grants Pass: Rogue Community College abandoned its paralegal program because the availability of jobs was very poor in the area, and those who did get them were usually expected to serve the dual function of legal secretary and paralegal. Starting salaries are low, too, ranging from $6000 to $8400.

PENNSYLVANIA

Allentown: A 1976 survey of forty-three law firms found that thirteen employed paralegals and eleven planned to hire some. Nineteen had no plans to use paralegals in the immediate future. This survey, although dated, is cited to show that even several years ago Allentown had a progressive attitude toward the paralegal profession. Employment opportunities are good here.

Chester: Average starting salaries are $8500 to $10,500. No information was received about the availability of jobs.

Harrisburg: A good job market. The state government alone employs about 200 paralegals. The Harrisburg Area Community College reports requests for job referrals from the district attorney's office, local banks, and a utilities company. Many private law firms in Harrisburg also employ paralegals at starting salaries ranging from $8500 to $10,000. State civil-service jobs pay up to $15,000.

Philadelphia: The Philadelphia Association of Paralegals made an extensive survey in 1975, whose results were published in 1976. A follow-up survey of salaries only was made in 1977 and published in 1978. As the first is too dated, there is no point in repeating its findings. The second showed that most starting salaries for the past several years had hovered around $9000. With one to three years experience, $11,000 to $12,000 was the most common salary. With over three years experience the average salary was $15,000, with two reporting over $16,000. The association had no job-market data, but the Institute for Paralegal Training in Philadelphia reports that it places 85 percent of its graduates through its own placement service.

Pittsburgh: The Pittsburgh Paralegal Association conducted a recent survey of area paralegals. Starting salaries ranged from $7000 to $13,000. Current salaries went up to $16,000. Data about job availability was not reported.

Summerdale: The Central Pennsylvania Business School reports an 82-percent placement rate for its paralegal graduates, with starting salaries ranging from $7500 to $8200.

RHODE ISLAND

In the major cities paralegal jobs start at $9000 to $11,000. There is currently little competition for jobs because only one school in Rhode Island conducts a paralegal course, and it has turned out only a few graduates.

SOUTH CAROLINA

No information is available.

SOUTH DAKOTA

Since no schools in this state offer paralegal training, and there are no paralegal associations, it may be assumed that the job market, if any, is poor.

TENNESSEE

See MISSISSIPPI for a report on Memphis. No other data is available.

TEXAS

Corpus Christi: Good job opportunities, with starting salaries of from $9000 to $10,200.

Dallas: Excellent job opportunities were reported by two different sources. One reported starting salaries at from $10,000 to $15,000; the other reported an overall salary range of from $9000 to $18,000.

El Paso: A recent survey showed that thirty new paralegal jobs per year were developing at starts of from $6500 to $8500.

Houston: The job market is good here, and getting better. Jobs are available both in law firms and in the legal departments of large oil companies. Starting salaries average $11,000. One paralegal, after seven years with a petroleum chemical company, reported a $20,000 salary. The Texas Paralegal School reports a great number of openings at starts of from $10,800 to $12,000.

UTAH

No information is available.

VERMONT

Montpelier: Woodbury Associates School of Continuing and Legal Education reports that most graduates of its one-year course are able to find paralegal work within the state, some in private law firms, but most in the public sector. No salary data were reported.

No information about other parts of the state was received.

VIRGINIA

No information is available.

WASHINGTON

A Washington Commission for Vocational Educators survey showed current employment of paralegals throughout the state at about 6200 persons. The outlook for both new jobs and replacements up through 1983 range between 500 and 525 openings a year.

Seattle: The Washington Legal Assistants Association, headquartered in Seattle, says that paralegal job openings in the area seem not to be advertised, but nevertheless are available. They recommend submitting resumés to law firms. A 1978 survey of the Seattle area showed a low salary of approximately $6900, a high of about $19,100, and a mean of about $12,450.

Tacoma: Job opportunities are limited for paralegals with no experience and less than a four-year college degree. One reason is that the University of Puget Sound Law School supplies many legal interns to law offices in the area, and these compete for jobs with paralegals. Those paralegals who manage to find jobs earn from $10,200 to $13,200.

WEST VIRGINIA

The West Virginia State Bar Association conducted a statewide survey of attorneys to assess the need for paralegals. The response was so overwhelmingly positive that the program at Marshall University in Huntington was instituted as a direct result. In the Huntington and Charleston areas, salaries start between $9000 and $10,000. With experience they range up to $16,000. There is no difficulty getting jobs.

WISCONSIN

No information is available.

WYOMING

As this state has no schools offering paralegal training and no paralegal associations, it may be assumed that the job market, if any, is poor.

8

The Paralegal Associations

Paralegal associations come and go. Some are firmly enough established. A few are even permanent enough to hire paid executive secretaries. But many are so ephemeral that they are here today and gone tomorrow.

A group of paralegals will get together to form a local association, and one will volunteer to handle the mail. The association address will then be in care of the law firm for which the volunteer works. Then he or she will switch jobs, the old firm won't bother to forward mail addressed to the association, and the organization will disappear into limbo.

I wrote to more than sixty paralegal associations across the country. Some letters came back stamped MOVED— LEFT NO FORWARDING ADDRESS. Others simply were not answered. As I had no way of knowing whether or not those in the latter category were still in existence, I have not listed them. Twenty-four paralegal associations were definitely still in existence.

NATIONAL ASSOCIATIONS

American Paralegal Association
Deborah Larbalestrier, Executive Director
P.O. Box 35223
Los Angeles, CA 90035
This organization, which does not appear to be very active, seems mainly concerned with attempting to get a code of ethics for paralegals adopted nationally.

National Association of Legal Assistants, Inc.
Marge L. Dover, Executive Director
3005 East Skelly Drive, Suite 122
Tulsa, OK 74105
This organization works to set standards for paralegals, and has devised a widely recognized "certification" test. It also organizes seminars for paralegals across the country.

National Federation of Paralegal Associations
Jeanne Kowalski, Executive Director
Ben Franklin Station
P.O. Box 14103
Washington, D.C.
This organization is just what its title suggests, a federation of paralegal associations across the country. Most firmly established state and local associations belong to it.

National Paralegal Institute, Inc.
2000 P St. NW, 6th Floor
Washington, D.C. 20036

This organization receives grants and contracts to design and deliver training to paralegals in public law subjects. It does not operate a school, but conducts special training events around the country upon the request of federal or state agencies.

STATE AND LOCAL ASSOCIATIONS

Members of the National Federation of Paralegal Associations are designated by an asterisk (*).

*East Bay Association of Legal Assistants
Jane Lamont, President
P.O. Box 424
Oakland, CA 94604

*Los Angeles Paralegal Association
Cheri Wilkinson, President
P.O. Box 24350
Los Angeles, CA 90024

*San Francisco Association of Legal Assistants
P.O. Box 26668
San Francisco, CA 94126

*Rocky Mountain Legal Assistants Association
Nancy Andreas, Secretary
P.O. Box 304
Denver, CO 80201

Connecticut Association of Paralegals
Joan Baird, President
P.O. Box 134
Bridgeport, CT 06601

*National Capitol Area Paralegal Association
P.O. Box 19505
Washington, D.C. 20036

*The Georgia Association of Legal Assistants
P.O. Box 1802
Atlanta, GA 30301

Hawaii Association of Legal Assistants
Frances M. White, President
P.O. Box 674
Honolulu, HI 96809

*Illinois Paralegal Association
Geri E. Rice, President
P.O. Box 857
Chicago, IL 60690

Kansas Legal Assistants Society
c/o Laurine R. Kreipe
8129 SE 2nd St.
Tecumseh, KS 66542

Louisiana Paralegal Association
c/o Joyce E. Ludwig
Sessions, Fishman, Rosenson, Snellings, & Boisfontaine
Attorneys and Counsellors at Law
Twenty-first Floor, the Bank of New Orleans Bldg.
1010 Common St.
New Orleans, LA 70112

*Massachusetts Paralegal Association
Kathleen H. Wade, President
P.O. Box 423
Boston, MA 02102

*Minnesota Association of Legal Assistants
P.O. Box 3712
Main Post Office
St. Paul, MN 55165

*Kansas City Association of Legal Assistants
Judith K. Wonn, President
P.O. Box 13223
Kansas City, MO 64199

*New York City Paralegal Association
P.O. Box 5143
FDR Station
New York, NY 10022

*Cleveland Association of Paralegals
Susan F. Timmerman, Secretary
P.O. Box 95527
Cleveland, OH 44113

*Philadelphia Association of Paralegals
Patricia A. Weeks, President
P.O. Box 55
Philadelphia, PA 19105

Pittsburgh Paralegal Association
Ellen Fenstermacher, Secretary
P.O. Box 1053
Pittsburgh, PA 15230

*Dallas Association of Legal Assistants
Jean M. Guzzetta, President
P.O. Box 50812
Dallas, TX 75250

*Washington Legal Assistants Association
 Robin R. Knudson
 P.O. Box 2114
 Seattle, WA 98111

Index